Fat Witch
Bake Sale

Fat Witch
Bake Sale

67 RECIPES FROM THE BELOVED
FAT WITCH BAKERY
FOR YOUR NEXT BAKE SALE OR PARTY

PATRICIA HELDING
WITH LUCY BAKER

PHOTOGRAPHY BY ALEXANDRA GRABLEWSKI

RODALE.

Rodale books may be purchased for business or promotional use or for special sales. For information, please write to: Special Markets Department, Rodale Inc. 733 Third Avenue, New York, NY 10017

Printed in the United States of America

Rodale Inc. makes every effort to use acid-free ♾ recycled paper ♻.

Photographs by Alexandra Grablewski

Book design by Joanna Williams

Library of Congress Cataloging-in-Publication Data is on file with the publisher.

ISBN 978–1–62336–226–3

Distributed to the trade by Macmillan

2   4   6   8   10   9   7   5   3   1   hardcover

We inspire and enable people to improve their lives and the world around them.

rodalebooks.com

THIS BOOK IS DEDICATED TO
ERIKA, CALVIN, MADISON, MARISSA,
CLAIRE, MORGAN, AND ANDY.

contents

introduction

Owning a successful bakery right smack in the middle of Manhattan is a bit like running a giant, crazy bake sale every single day. Only instead of a card table overflowing with platters of cupcakes, zip-top bags filled with chocolate chip cookies, and foil pie plates stacked with Rice Krispies Treats, at Fat Witch Bakery we have an entire store filled with the most luscious, irresistible brownies you can imagine: Fudgy chocolate, gooey caramel, tart dried cherry, and chewy oatmeal-walnut are just a few variations in our regular rotation. We certainly produce more than your average fund-raiser—7,500-plus brownies a day. But the central concepts of a good bake sale and our bakery are the same: to make money by offering people delicious desserts made with honest ingredients and prepared with love.

People often ask me for business advice. But the truth is, I didn't set out to own a bakery. Never in a million years did I imagine that my humble brownies would become the object of obsession for throngs of New Yorkers and hungry tourists. In fact, I started out as a trader on Wall Street. Exhausted and weary at the end of each day, I sought solace in butter, flour, and chocolate. By concentrating on the simple acts of mixing ingredients, pouring them into a pan, and sliding them into a hot oven, I was able to unwind and forget the ups and downs of the stock market.

Though it began as a casual hobby, I quickly became obsessed with creating the perfect brownie recipe. I wanted my brownies to be beyond sensational—rich and chocolatey, with a moist, tender crumb and a glossy, ever-so-crackly top. Every time I tested a new version, I brought the results to work the next day. Traders are notorious for cutting straight to the chase; I knew they wouldn't hesitate to give me a bull or bear response. After many attempts (and countless eggs, sticks of butter, and bags of chocolate chips!), success: My colleagues finally gave me a "double thumbs-up." I had achieved brownie nirvana.

Somewhere along the way, I realized that my true calling wasn't the stock market—it was baking. Even though I had no experience, I decided to open my own business. Inspired? Yes. Insane? Perhaps. When I first started out, I didn't even know what a convection oven was, and I used a pancake griddle to seal cellophane around those first batches of Witches.

But knowing next to nothing about commercial baking had advantages. It left me open to improvisation and forced me to think outside the 9" x 9" pan. In 1998, I found space inside Chelsea Market, the former Nabisco factory building and the place where Oreo cookies were invented. In the beginning, we did all the baking, packaging, and selling out of a tiny area. Now we have a much larger production site on

Park Avenue in East Harlem. We bake thousands of brownies a day and ship them all over the United States.

At the bakery, everything is done on big commercial equipment. But at home, in my minuscule Manhattan apartment kitchen, I still bake with my old handheld mixer, a timer shaped like a rooster, and my favorite mixing bowl, brought back from a trip to Tokyo. The recipes for this book come from my own index card file and were baked in my own home oven. These are the desserts that I prepare for my family and friends. Of course, there are lots of brownies, like pecan caramel, red velvet, yogurt, and—yes—bacon, but there are also cookies, bars, cupcakes, and cakes. Most of the recipes are kid friendly, but there are a few adults-only treats (Kahlúa–Chocolate Chip Cookies, anyone?). I've also included special chapters for gluten-free and vegan treats, like Toffee-Chocolate Chunks and Orange–Pine Nut Cookies. Everything travels well and most need no refrigeration, so they're all pretty much bake sale ready.

In addition to the recipes in this book, I share my expertise about running a profitable baking business: the marketing tips it took me years to learn, techniques for staying organized and delegating tasks, as well as ideas for packaging and staging your baked goods for maximum selling effect. Trust me, when you regularly orchestrate the delivery of half a ton of sugar, 500 pounds of chocolate, and giant 55-pound cubes of butter, you know a little bit about stocking a kitchen with everything you need for bake sale success!

I wish you good luck with your bake sale. I know it is for a great cause. Armed with my tried-and-true recipes and expert advice, you are sure to have a smashing success.

baKing basics

Ingredients

Nothing takes the wind out of my (bake) "sails" quite like realizing I have to buy some expensive, hard-to-find ingredient to use in just one recipe. To that end, I've made every effort to ensure that most of the ingredients called for in this book can be purchased at your local supermarket. (I push a shopping cart down a grocery store aisle just like you do!) I confess that there are a few obscure ingredients here, but I emphasize the word *few*. I started out as a home baker, and two of the best things about my recipes are how uncomplicated they are to make and how basic the ingredients are. That said, any brownie, cookie, or cupcake is only as good as the sum of its parts. Here are some helpful ingredient tips.

Butter: All of these recipes call for unsalted butter. If you are in a pinch and need to use salted butter, just omit the salt from the rest of the recipe. To soften butter quickly, dice it into small pieces, spread them on a plate, and leave it on the counter for about 30 minutes.

Eggs: I use large eggs. Buy the freshest ones you can find.

Flour: I use unbleached all-purpose flour, but any good, all-purpose flour will work. To measure flour, fluff it up with the measuring cup and then "spoon and sweep," brushing the excess off the top.

Sugar: Use any good-quality white granulated cane sugar. Light and dark brown sugar, when called for, should be gently packed into the measuring cup or spoon to ensure accurate results. If you absolutely must, you can substitute light brown sugar for dark brown, but your dessert won't have quite the same depth of flavor. Never make substitutions for confectioners' sugar.

Vanilla extract: Pure vanilla extract is a must. My favorite comes from Madagascar. It's expensive, I know, but take a deep breath and splurge. It's well worth it. Never use vanilla flavoring.

Cocoa powder: I use natural, unsweetened cocoa powder (not Dutch process). Any good-quality supermarket brand is fine.

Chocolate: Most of the recipes in this book start with either unsweetened chocolate (100% cacao) or bittersweet chocolate (60% to 85% cacao). Use whatever brand you prefer. I often use Ghirardelli, an all-American chocolate. When a recipe calls for white chocolate, make sure that it contains some cocoa butter.

Tools

Bake sale treats should entice and impress, but they should be homey and familiar, too. Don't feel like you need to spend a fortune on mini–Bundt pans, pastry bags for piping frosting, and other specialty kitchen gadgets. At the bakery, we have lots of fancy culinary tools, but at home, I bake with the same basic equipment that you do.

Here is a secret: I don't even own a stand mixer! I have used the same handheld electric mixer for as long as I can remember, and it works like a charm.

Here is a short list of basic baking tools you'll need to make this book's recipes.

Measuring cups for dry ingredients	Mixing bowls	9" x 9" baking pan
Clear measuring cup for liquid ingredients	Medium whisk	One 9" x 5" loaf pan
Measuring spoons	Electric mixer	One 8" x 4" loaf pan
Medium-size, flexible, heatproof spatula	Sharp knife	Two 9" round cake pans
Wire cooling rack	Small and medium heavy-bottom saucepans	One madeleine pan
Wooden spoon	Two large 18" x 13" baking sheets or jelly roll pans	One mini muffin pan
		Parchment paper
		Aluminum foil

Tips for Great Results

Baking is a science, but there is a little magic in it, too. I slide a pan full of batter or a tray of dough into the oven and cross my fingers and hold my breath, hoping that what emerges is transformed into a perfectly luscious batch of brownies or tender-crisp cookies, smelling of warm butter and sugar. Here are some helpful tips to ensure showstopping results every time.

Read the recipe through from start to finish before you begin. Nothing is worse than realizing right in the middle of things that you are short an egg or that you preheated the oven to the wrong temperature.

Know your oven. None is exactly like another. Start testing your treats for doneness 5 minutes before the time stated in the recipe. That way, you'll be sure not to overbake. The best way to test if a batch of brownies or bars is done is to stick a toothpick in the center. It should come out with a few moist crumbs attached. Cookies are done when the edges are crisp and golden and the centers are still a bit soft.

Learn to melt chocolate like a pro. If you are using a whole bar, chop it into small, equal-size pieces with a knife. Put the pieces in a heatproof bowl and microwave on medium power for 20- to 30-second increments, stirring between each one, until almost all of the chocolate is melted. Take the bowl out of the microwave oven and stir until the chocolate is completely melted and smooth. You can also melt chocolate in a heatproof bowl set over a pan of gently simmering water or in a small heavy-bottom saucepan over low heat. Just be careful and stir constantly. Chocolate, and especially white chocolate, seizes and burns quickly.

Let melted chocolate and butter cool before mixing them into the batter. If they are too hot, they could start to cook the eggs.

For easy cleanup when baking brownies and bars, line the pan with foil along the bottom and up the sides. That way, you can remove the entire contents at once. It also makes for easier cutting.

Resist the urge to dive right in. As hard as it is to wait, your treats need to cool before you indulge. Cutting brownies or bars too soon leads to messy edges and lots of broken pieces.

welcome to your bake sale

There is no question that a bake sale is a fun event. What's not to love about a community gathering centered around Red Velvet–Milk Chocolate Brownies, Cinnamon Toast Bars, and Coconut–Macadamia Nut Cookies? But running a successful bake sale also requires a lot of effort, planning, organization, and mediation. Things can get a little tricky when you have to supervise people with whom you have a personal relationship, like the soccer coach, your child's best friend's mom, or the star singer from your church's choir. From early brainstorming sessions to the main event, here are some helpful hints, tips, and ideas to ensure that your bake sale goes off without a hitch.

Before the Event

Decide on a date, time, and location, and make sure you have permission to hold your bake sale.

Don't allow too many cooks in the kitchen. Bake sales also need people in charge of donations, setup, cleanup, and manning the cash box. Make sure all participants are clear about their roles.

Communicate. Hold a meeting to plan your sale. Setting up a group e-mail list is also a good way to keep everyone up-to-date and informed. Be clear about whether or not you will reach out to your personal and business contacts.

Define the "rules" of your bake sale. If it's at an elementary school, do the baked goods have to be nut free? Should everything be homemade, or are bags of jelly beans okay?

Clearly state the purpose of your bake sale. It's important to identify what you are raising money for. Be as specific as possible: The Little League team needs new uniforms; the local animal shelter wants to build a dog run; your temple would like to purchase new books for Hebrew school.

Give your bake sale a theme. Instead of the "Lincoln School Bake Sale," think: "Shiver your timbers at the Lincoln School Pirate Bake Sale! All booty from the treasure chest will be contributed to the school's art program." Here are a few ideas: seasonal (summer, fall, winter, spring); holidays (Halloween, Thanksgiving, Hanukkah, Christmas, Valentine's Day, Saint Patrick's Day, Purim, Easter, July 4th); international (treats from all over the world); regional goodies (New England baked goods, southern favorites); heirloom family recipes; chocolate lovers (everything chocolate); the Olympics/sports; Mother's or Father's Day; Broadway (desserts on stage!). The possibilities are endless.

Utilize social media. Publicize your bake sale via Facebook, Twitter, Instagram, Pinterest, and YouTube. Update these sites frequently with pictures, recipes, and fun baking facts.

Make signs. Children's art and handwriting are at the top of the charm chart. Vintage photographs of local attractions are also a good bet. In a pinch, clip art or stock photos will work just fine. Create the signs yourself, or see if a graphic designer will do it at no cost. In exchange, offer to display the designer's business cards near the event's cash register. Post the signs in local shops and businesses at least 1 week prior to the event.

Ask for donations. Each year, Fat Witch donates lots of brownies to New York City public school bake sales. Here's what is effective with most businesses.

- **Check out the FAQs on the business's/bakery's Web site.** Often there is information about donations or charitable giving. Also check out the "Contact Us" section. If you don't follow the Web site's directions, you might not get a response.
- **Contact the business 4 to 8 weeks ahead of time.** Be specific and be reasonable. In the body of your short letter/e-mail/phone call, let the company know a little bit about the charity, the date of the event, how many people you expect, and what would be the ideal donation. Never send more than one attachment.
- **If you don't hear from the business,** limit your follow-up to no more than two calls/e-mails/letters. Understand that no means no, and no response could also mean no.

- **Have your tax-exempt form ready** to e-mail, fax, or mail.

- **If your event is near a holiday,** a local business may not be able to donate. Consider asking for a gift certificate instead. If your state allows gift certificate expiration dates, make it known at the event that there is a time limit on the certificate's redemption.

- **Ask about purchasing at a discount.** This can be almost as good as getting a free donation. Everyone makes some money, and the bakery/business doesn't feel pushed to the wall.

- **Think outside the oven.** You'll probably need small bags, waxed paper, paper plates, plastic forks, napkins, cake boxes, vinyl gloves, boxes, hand trucks, and garbage bags. These things might be more easily donated by your local bakery than actual baked goods.

- **Think about display needs.** A local florist could donate an arrangement; a hardware store could lend wooden planks to be placed between ladder steps or on file cabinets; a kitchen supply store could lend you trays or standing grid panels with clamps for display.

- **If you pick up the donation,** you've taken a burden off the vendor. At Fat Witch Bakery, we have an absolute rule: We donate; you pick up.

- **A word to the wise: Be sure to say thank-you.** You should always credit the business at the event by putting its logo and name on social media and signage at the sale, if possible. A thank-you after the event is a must. A note with a photo from the bake sale keeps it on a personal (dare I say charming?) level. E-mail also works.

The Big Day

I hate to say it, but at first glance, most bake sales look rather bland: three folding tables covered with cheap plastic tablecloths, laden with an uninspired display of treats on a mishmash of plates. There are no decorations; no flowers, balloons, or pops of color. It's such a shame! With just a little effort, you can make your bake sale look as good as it tastes—and you'll be surprised at how much faster your cash box fills up.

Choose a color scheme. Bold color catches and holds the eye, so don't be shy. Think fuchsia over baby pink, gold over pale yellow. Make sure your colors match your theme (orange and black for Halloween, blue and silver for Hanukkah, etc.).

Decorate. Ask local schools for student artwork. Use it to make flyers and also display it at the bake sale to create a fun and warm environment.

Create different levels. At Fat Witch, we display our brownies on trays, in baskets, on cake stands, and on shelves. When everything is at the same height, it looks amateurish. Don't worry—you don't have to invest in fancy display pieces. Cover a few cardboard boxes in gift wrap, put a child's step stool on the table, or repurpose last year's Easter baskets.

Package some of the baked goods. Cute bags, pretty ribbon, and paper containers are available online and in party stores. You'll be surprised how attractive your treats will be with a minimum of decorative effort.

This is dessert, not math! Make pricing easy. Have everything divisible by 25 cents, and keep a calculator near each cash box.

Consider offering special deals such as one cupcake for $1 and three for $2.50. It's an effective upsell.

List the ingredients of each baked good. This is especially helpful for those who want to avoid allergens.

Keep a stack of paper plates and napkins, along with plastic forks and spoons, handy for folks who want to dive right in. Also make sure to have plenty of bags and bakery boxes for people who want to take their treats home. Don't forget trash bins!

Hopefully there won't be a single crumb remaining, but make a plan for leftovers. See if you can donate them to a local charity.

Figure out how the trash will be dealt with—and decide this before the event. If you are holding your bake sale at a facility that has people on staff to do this job, certainly tip them and give thanks. Either way, organize a cleanup crew and make sure they stick around until the job is done. It's important to have more than one person responsible for breaking down the setup and taking trash to the receptacles.

Check with your local health department about any food safety permits you may need.

And the Day After

Remember to thank everyone involved, whether they were major players from start to finish or they simply donated a few necessary items. If you have an especially large number of people to thank, a form letter or e-mail is okay. Create your message before the bake sale so it's ready to be sent out the day after the event. Give a shout-out on social media, too. At Fat Witch, we buddy up with charities that tweet about us, who like us on Facebook and Pinterest and acknowledge the donation. A little thanks goes a long ways toward sweet success at your next bake sale fund-raiser.

Chocolate
Chocolate
Chocolate

chocolate, chocolate, chocolate

Every bake sale should include a mix of new flavors as well as classic treats, and chocolate is always a surefire hit. Who can resist cocoa-infused cookies studded with milk chocolate chunks, luscious red velvet brownies slathered with cream cheese frosting, or a thick slice of mile-high triple-layer chocolate layer cake? No one I've ever met, that's for sure. At Fat Witch, we go through mountains of chocolate every week, and people just keep coming back for more.

In fact, I would argue that chocolate plays a pivotal role in the lives of many Americans. It has always topped the charts as our most favorite flavor. As far back as World War I, the US Army supplied troops with chocolate bars to eat for a quick pick-me-up.

19

Even if you've never spent 1 minute in boot camp, you've probably grabbed a candy bar (or two or three) on the go. Chocolate is important for special occasions, too. What would Valentine's Day be without that fancy box of bonbons? Hanukkah without the gold foil–covered gelt? Or an extravagant wedding reception without the chocolate fountain?

I remember the intense pleasure of savoring a Hershey's bar as a child: ripping off the paper, breaking apart each individual rectangle, and letting the pieces melt into creamy puddles on my tongue. I ate only milk chocolate, because that was the one kind available on the supermarket shelf. Today's chocoholics have it much better: From bitter to silky sweet, pure white to blackest black, chocolate encompasses a vast range of flavors. Even though I love all kinds of chocolate, most of my recipes begin with unsweetened or bittersweet, which provides the most intense chocolate notes in the finished dessert.

Since chocolate treats are guaranteed to fly off your bake sale table, why not create a special display? Decorate it with a chocolate-colored tablecloth, boxes of cocoa, and glass bowls filled with white and dark chocolate chips. This chapter contains my most indulgent, over-the-top chocolate treats, from homey brownies and cupcakes to thumbprint cookies. Be forewarned: You might want to bake double batches to keep some for yourself!

pecan-caramel brownies

Our Chelsea Market bakery is perfectly situated within New York's famous Nabisco building, just beyond the main entrance. Hundreds of office workers pass by each day on their way to and from work. Starting around 5:00 p.m., these brownies tend to fly off the shelf. I think the combination of crunchy pecans, sticky caramel, and coarse sea salt is especially hard to resist after a long daily grind.

BROWNIE BASE

- 12 tablespoons (1½ sticks) unsalted butter
- 4 ounces bittersweet chocolate, chopped into small, even-size pieces
- 3 large eggs
- 1 cup + 1 tablespoon granulated sugar
- 1 teaspoon pure vanilla extract
- ½ cup unbleached all-purpose flour
- Pinch of salt
- ½ cup pecans, coarsely chopped

TOPPING

- 40 caramel candy squares
- 2½ tablespoons lukewarm water (90°–95°F)
- ½ cup pecans, coarsely chopped
- 1 tablespoon coarse sea salt (optional)

1. Preheat the oven to 350°F. Grease a 9" x 9" baking pan with butter or cooking spray. Dust with flour and tap out the excess.

2. *To make the brownie base:* In a small heavy-bottom saucepan over low heat, warm the butter and chocolate, stirring frequently, until almost completely melted. Remove the saucepan from the heat and stir until smooth. Set aside and cool slightly.

3. In a large bowl, using an electric mixer, beat the eggs, sugar, and vanilla until creamy. Add the cooled chocolate mixture and mix until well combined.

4. Measure the flour and salt and sift directly into the chocolate mixture. Mix completely. Stir in the pecans.

5. Pour the batter into the prepared pan and spread evenly with a spatula. Bake for 30 to 35 minutes, or until a toothpick inserted into the center comes out clean or with only crumbs, not batter, on it. Cool in the pan on a rack for at least 2 hours.

6. *To make the topping:* Unwrap the caramel squares and put them in a microwaveable bowl. Add the water and microwave on medium power, checking every 60 seconds, until the caramels have melted into a thick liquid. Set aside for 3 to 5 minutes, until slightly cooled. Whisk the caramel with a fork until it is completely smooth. With the fork, drizzle the caramel back and forth over the top of the brownies. While the caramel is still soft, sprinkle the brownies with the pecans and salt, if desired.

TIP

Pretty trays make baked goods look even more delectable.

7. Put the pan in the refrigerator to set the caramel, pecans, and salt. Keep chilled until ready to serve. Cut just before serving or wrapping for the bake sale.

Storage: *The brownies will keep longer if they are stored uncut. Cover the pan tightly with plastic wrap or foil and store in the refrigerator for 6 to 8 days.*

chocolate layer cake

There are moments in life when nothing should get between you and your chocolate, unless it's a delectable layer of icing. Even though I'm a brownie baker, chocolate cake has a special place in my heart. At home, I usually make this as a two-layer cake, but for a bake sale, I think a three-layer cake is much more impressive. It's sure to elicit plenty of oohs and aahs—not to mention plenty of sales!

The beauty of the recipe is that it is easily doubled or tripled (or quadrupled!), so you can make as many layers as you want. I usually frost this with White Chocolate Frosting (page 173), but check out the rest of the icings in Chapter 10—any of them would be delicious.

1. Preheat the oven to 350°F. Grease as many 9" round cake pans (or 9" x 9" baking pans) as you plan to have layers with butter or cooking spray, making sure to get the sides. Dust with flour and tap out the excess. Set the pan(s) aside. *Make sure you double or triple the recipe ingredients if you want more than 1 layer.*

2. In a large bowl, using an electric mixer, cream the sugar and eggs until light and fluffy. Add the vanilla. Add the milk and beat to combine. Beat in the oil. Measure the cocoa and sift directly into the bowl. (It's important to sift the cocoa to prevent lumps.) Beat until well combined.

3. Measure the flour, salt, baking powder, and baking soda and sift directly into the batter. Blend just until incorporated.

4. Spread the batter evenly into the prepared pan(s) and bake for 28 to 32 minutes, or until a toothpick inserted in the center comes out clean or with only crumbs, not batter, on it. Cool in the pan(s) on a rack for at least 1 hour. Turn the cake out onto a plate and cool completely before icing.

Storage: *To store the frosted cake, stick a few toothpicks into the top and cover with plastic wrap (the toothpicks will keep the frosting from smearing). The cake will keep at room temperature for 3 to 4 days or in the refrigerator for 5 to 7 days.*

1 cup granulated sugar
2 large eggs
1/2 teaspoon pure vanilla extract
1/3 cup whole milk
1/4 cup flavorless vegetable oil
1/3 cup unsweetened cocoa powder
1 cup unbleached all-purpose flour
1/2 teaspoon salt
1/2 teaspoon baking powder
1/2 teaspoon baking soda

Tip

The great bake sale debate is whether to cut cakes into pieces or sell them by the half or whole. My suggestion is to make one cake for slices and another to sell in halves or quarters.

turbo-chocolate cookies

makes 24 to 36 cookies

A bake sale without cookies is like a circus without an elephant, a football team without a quarter-back, a canoe without paddles . . . you get the idea. One of the great things about these drop cookies (other than the loads of chocolate) is that you can make them any size you want. I like to bake jumbo cookies using tablespoons to scoop the dough. But you could also use teaspoons and sell bags of "one-bite" cookies. If you do bake mini-cookies, just be sure to reduce the baking time by a few minutes.

This recipe is one of my favorites. When I bake it at home, I've been known to bust out my fancy crystal goblets and pour my guests glasses of milk for dunking.

You may need to bake these in batches if you don't have more than one cookie sheet.

---

1. Preheat the oven to 350°F. Grease 2 large baking sheets with butter or cooking spray or line them with parchment paper.

2. In a large bowl, using an electric mixer, beat the butter, eggs, granulated sugar, and brown sugar until frothy. Add the vanilla and continue to beat until smooth and well combined.

3. Measure the confectioners' sugar, flour, cocoa, baking powder, and salt and sift directly into the butter mixture. Mix well until no trace of the dry ingredients remains. Stir in the chocolate chips.

4. Using 2 tablespoons and working in batches if needed, drop balls of dough onto the prepared baking sheets, making sure to space them at least 1" apart.

5. Bake for 10 to 14 minutes, or until the edges are crisp and the centers are no longer shiny. Cool on the baking sheets on a rack for at least 20 minutes. Remove the cookies to a serving platter and repeat with the remaining cookie dough.

Storage: The cookies will keep for a week stored in an airtight container at room temperature.

12 tablespoons (1½ sticks) unsalted butter, room temperature

2 large eggs

⅓ cup granulated sugar

⅓ cup packed dark brown sugar

1 teaspoon pure vanilla extract

5 tablespoons confectioners' sugar

1¼ cups unbleached all-purpose flour

½ cup unsweetened cocoa powder

½ teaspoon baking powder

½ teaspoon salt

½ cup semisweet chocolate chips

Tip Cookies are perfect upsell items—for instance, one for 50 cents and three for $1.

raise the chocolate bar

Do you know that ubiquitous football-party appetizer? The dip with layer upon layer of beans, cheese, guacamole, and sour cream? Well, that was the inspiration for these bars—only instead of tortilla chips, these treats are all about chocolate. They aren't difficult to make, but they do require a bit of extra effort. Trust me, the results are absolutely worth it. A rich brownie base is coated with bittersweet chocolate, which is spread with Nutella, which is then covered with semisweet chocolate chips and drizzled with white chocolate. Whew! Got all that?

These bars are so gorgeous and irresistible, I guarantee they will be one of the first things to sell out at your bake sale. And you might just inspire a fan club.

BROWNIE BASE

- 6 tablespoons unsalted butter
- 3 ounces bittersweet chocolate (60% cacao content works best), chopped into small, even-size pieces
- ¾ cup granulated sugar
- 2 large eggs
- ½ teaspoon pure vanilla extract
- ⅓ cup unbleached all-purpose flour
- Pinch of salt

LAYERS

- 4 ounces bittersweet chocolate (80% cacao), chopped into small, even-size pieces
- 1 cup (8 ounces) Nutella
- ½ cup semisweet chocolate chips
- ⅓ cup white chocolate chips

1. Preheat the oven to 350°F. Tightly line the bottom and sides of a 9" x 9" baking pan with foil.

2. *To make the brownie base:* In a small heavy-bottom saucepan over low heat, warm the butter and bittersweet chocolate, stirring frequently, until almost completely melted. Remove the saucepan from the heat and stir until completely smooth. Set aside to cool slightly.

3. In a large bowl, using an electric mixer, beat the sugar, eggs, and vanilla together until smooth. Add the cooled chocolate mixture and stir to combine.

4. Measure the flour and salt and sift together directly into the chocolate mixture. Mix gently until well blended and no trace of the dry ingredients remains. Spread the brownie batter evenly in the prepared pan and bake for 18 minutes, or until a toothpick inserted in the center comes out clean or with only crumbs, not batter, on it. Cool in the pan on a rack for 1 hour. Flip the pan over onto a large, flat plate and remove the foil.

5. *To make the layers:* Put the bittersweet chocolate in a microwaveable bowl and microwave on medium power, stirring every 20 to 30 seconds, until almost completely melted. Stir until smooth. Set

aside for 5 minutes, until slightly cooled. Spread the melted chocolate evenly on top of the brownie base. Refrigerate for 15 minutes.

6. Spread the Nutella over the bittersweet chocolate layer. Toss the semisweet chips evenly on top. Return to the refrigerator and chill for 15 minutes.

7. Put the white chocolate in a microwaveable bowl and microwave on medium power, stirring every 30 seconds, until almost completely melted. Stir until smooth. Set aside for 3 to 5 minutes, until slightly cooled. Drizzle the white chocolate over the top of the brownie bars. Refrigerate for 5 to 10 minutes to set the white chocolate. Cut into bars. Refrigerate until ready to serve or until just before the bake sale.

Storage: *Cover the pan with plastic wrap or foil and store in the refrigerator for 5 to 7 days.*

red velvet–milk chocolate brownies

Fried chicken. Sweet tea. Pralines. There's no denying that the South is home to some of America's greatest culinary traditions. And red velvet cake is certainly no exception. Its sultry ruby hue and subtle chocolate flavor (made all the better with a slick of cream cheese frosting) has made it a favorite choice for sweet celebrations.

For this recipe, I use milk chocolate. I like its mild, creamy flavor, plus it really allows the red coloring to show through. Top these brownies with a Cream Cheese Schmear (page 170).

---

1. Preheat the oven to 350°F. Grease a 9" x 9" baking pan with butter or cooking spray. Dust with flour and tap out the excess.

2. In a small heavy-bottom saucepan over low heat, combine the butter, sugar, and milk. Stir until the mixture is melted and smooth. Remove the saucepan from the heat and add the chocolate chips. Stir until everything is completely melted. Transfer the chocolate mixture to a large mixing bowl. Add the eggs one at a time and mix until well combined.

3. Measure the flour, salt, and baking soda and sift directly into the chocolate mixture. Using an electric mixer on low speed, beat until no trace of the dry ingredients remains. Add the vanilla and food coloring and continue to beat on low speed until everything is thoroughly combined.

4. Pour the batter into the prepared pan and spread evenly with a spatula. Bake for 30 to 35 minutes, or until a toothpick inserted in the center comes out clean or with only crumbs, not batter, on it. Cool in the pan on a rack for at least 1 hour. If you are frosting the brownies, make sure they have cooled completely. Refrigerate until serving.

Storage: *The brownies will keep longer if they are stored uncut. Cover the pan tightly with plastic wrap or foil and, if iced, store in the refrigerator for 6 to 8 days.*

5½ tablespoons (⅓ cup) unsalted butter
¾ cup granulated sugar
2 tablespoons whole milk
1 cup milk chocolate chips
2 large eggs
¾ cup unbleached all-purpose flour
¼ teaspoon salt
¼ teaspoon baking soda
1 teaspoon pure vanilla extract
1 teaspoon red food coloring

TIP While delicious any time of the year, these are a must for a Valentine's Day bake sale. Dust the tops with red sprinkles or conversation hearts.

baby brownie cupcakes

Every bake sale needs a treat for those with tiny hands. What could be better than a miniature brownie-cupcake mash-up? These two-bite treats look like regular mini-cupcakes, but beneath that cap of frosting is an intense, fudgy brownie base. To gild the lily, garnish each one with a small piece of candy or with any of the topping ideas from Chapter 10, Over-the-Top Icings. A word to the wise: It's pretty much impossible to eat just one. If you don't have a mini-muffin pan, you can bake these in a regular muffin pan.

12 tablespoons (1½ sticks) unsalted butter

4 ounces bittersweet chocolate (60% cacao), chopped into small, even-size pieces

1¼ cups granulated sugar

3 large eggs

1 teaspoon pure vanilla extract

½ cup + 2 tablespoons unbleached all-purpose flour

Pinch of salt

Candy for topping (optional)

Tip

Consider a big platter or tray to display cupcakes.

1. Preheat the oven to 350°F. Fill a mini-muffin pan with paper liners.

2. In a small heavy-bottom saucepan over low heat, warm the butter and chocolate, stirring frequently, until almost completely melted. Remove the saucepan from the heat and stir until smooth. Set aside and cool slightly.

3. In a large bowl, using an electric mixer, mix the sugar, eggs, and vanilla together. Add the cooled chocolate mixture and mix until well blended.

4. Measure the flour and salt and sift directly into the chocolate mixture. Mix gently until well blended and no trace of the dry ingredients remains.

5. With a spoon, scoop the batter evenly into the paper liners and bake for 20 to 25 minutes, or until a toothpick inserted in the center comes out clean or with only crumbs, not batter, on it. Cool in the pan on a rack for 1 hour. Remove the brownies from the pan. Spread the top of each one with frosting, then, if desired, top with a piece of candy.

Storage: *Frosted cupcakes will keep at room temperature for 3 to 4 days or in the refrigerator for 6 to 8 days. Stick a toothpick in the top of each one and cover them with plastic wrap. This will keep the frosting from smearing.*

milk chocolate thumbprints

Carrot sticks, apple slices, and granola bars are all well and good, but my all-time favorite afternoon pick-me-up is a cookie. You would never sit down and eat a giant slice of cake 2 hours before dinner, but a cookie at 4:00 p.m.? Perfectly acceptable.

These are my all-time-favorite thumbprint cookies. Soft and chewy with a perfect bite of milk chocolate at the center, they taste as impressive as they look. They are sure to be a big hit with ravenous kids on their way home from school.

---

1. Preheat the oven to 350°F. Grease 2 large baking sheets with butter or cooking spray or line them with parchment paper.

2. In a small heavy-bottom saucepan over low heat, warm the butter and chopped chocolate, stirring frequently, until almost completely melted. Remove the saucepan from the heat and whisk in the cocoa. Set aside to cool for 3 to 5 minutes.

3. In a large bowl, using an electric mixer, beat the sugar, egg, and vanilla until creamy. Add the chocolate mixture and beat until well combined. Sift the flour, baking soda, and salt directly into the chocolate mixture and beat just until no trace of the dry ingredients remains.

4. Using a teaspoon, drop balls of dough onto the prepared baking sheets, making sure to space them at least 1½" apart. Using your thumb (it helps to wet it first) or the back of a spoon, make a small indentation in the center of each ball of dough and fill each with one large chocolate chip.

5. Bake the cookies for 9 to 12 minutes. Cool on the baking sheets on a rack for 20 minutes. Remove the cookies to the rack and cool completely.

Storage: *These cookies will keep for 5 to 7 days stored in an airtight container at room temperature.*

- 8 tablespoons (1 stick) unsalted butter
- 6 ounces milk chocolate, chopped into small, even-size pieces
- 1 tablespoon unsweetened cocoa powder, sifted
- ½ cup granulated sugar
- 1 large egg
- 1 teaspoon pure vanilla extract
- 1¼ cups unbleached all-purpose flour
- ½ teaspoon baking soda
- Big pinch of salt
- 36–48 large milk chocolate chips (the largest you can find)

Tip Glass jars are great for displaying cookies. Make certain the jar top is wide enough for cookies to slide out easily.

here's baking for you, Kids

Do you remember your favorite dessert from childhood? Unless your parents were pastry chefs, it probably wasn't a fussy baked Alaska, a fancy Sachertorte, or an impossible-to-make-at-home French macaron. Chances are you loved humble, easy favorites with familiar flavors: cinnamon toast, yellow cake, strawberry jam, and, of course, chocolate. From cookies and milk as an after-school snack to towering birthday cakes bedazzled with sprinkles, there's no doubt that kids love sweets. In fact, I'd say they go together like peanut butter and jelly or vanilla ice cream and warm brownies.

It's no surprise that one of the most common places for a bake sale is the schoolyard. It makes sense, then, to offer lots of kid-friendly treats at school bake sales.

(I'm a big proponent of catering to your audience!) The recipes in this chapter are devoted to time-honored ingredients adored by the younger set—and the young at heart.

These are also incredibly easy to prepare, making them a great choice for when you are baking with little helpers. Here are a few of my favorite tips for cooking with kids.

Have everything ready to go. Gather all the tools you need, grease the pan, and measure the ingredients into little bowls so kids can just dump and stir.

Embrace the mess. Working in the kitchen is not the time to wear your favorite sweater or use your grandmother's heirloom ceramic mixing bowl. Flour will fly and milk will spill—it's all part of the fun.

Show and tell. If kids are too young to use the electric mixer or wield a spatula, pull up a chair for them to stand on and watch. I guarantee they will find it fascinating.

Know when to step back and let them do it. As much as you want the finished product to look perfect, remind yourself that it's more important to let the kids do the frosting and decorating. If it's really important that your bake sale treats look just right, consider baking two batches.

Baking with kids is a great way to encourage them to unplug, work with their hands, and be creative. And no matter how lopsided the cake or lumpy the cookies, they will be proud of their work—and eager to eat it. Who knows, maybe one of your kids will grow up to be a pastry chef!

thumbprint blondies with jam

Baking thumbprint cookies is a childhood ritual. It's so much fun to use your fingers to shape the dough—for once, you actually get to play with your food!

When I was starting out as a home baker, I had only 1 cookie sheet. I had a desperate craving for thumbprints, but I didn't have enough time to bake round after round of batches. Instead, I created this recipe, which is essentially a thumbprint cookie in bar form.

I generally use raspberry preserves or apricot jam in these bars. Jelly won't work, because it will sink into the batter. I sometimes toss in a handful of roasted peanuts for a bit of crunch, but they are optional.

1. Preheat the oven to 350°F. Grease a 9" x 9" baking pan with butter or cooking spray. Dust with flour and tap out the excess.

2. In a large bowl, using an electric mixer, beat the butter and eggs until light and fluffy. Beat in the sugar and vanilla until well blended.

3. Measure the flour, salt, and baking soda and sift directly into the butter mixture. Beat just until combined.

4. Spread the batter evenly in the prepared pan. With a teaspoon, make 12 to 16 evenly spaced depressions in the batter. (If the spoon sticks, dip it in hot water.) Press hard enough so that the indentations reach halfway through the dough but not to the bottom of the pan. Fill each indentation with a scoop of jam or preserves. Sprinkle with the peanuts, if using.

5. Bake for 25 minutes, or until the top is golden and a toothpick inserted in the center comes out clean or with only crumbs, not batter, on it. Cool in the pan on a rack for 1 hour. Cut into bars just before serving.

Storage: *The blondies will keep longer uncut. Cover the pan tightly with plastic wrap or foil and store at room temperature for 1 to 3 days or in the refrigerator for 4 to 6 days.*

- 8 tablespoons (1 stick) unsalted butter, room temperature
- 2 large eggs
- 1¼ cups packed light brown sugar
- 2 teaspoons pure vanilla extract
- 1¾ cups unbleached all-purpose flour
- ½ teaspoon salt
- ¼ teaspoon baking soda
- ½ cup jam or preserves, such as raspberry, strawberry, or apricot
- ½ cup coarsely chopped skinned, roasted peanuts (optional)

Tip Individual containers are an eye-catching, "buy-me-now" enticement.

peanut butter brownies

There are lots of recipes for brownies with peanut butter swirls or peanut butter chips. Of course, they are delicious, but I always feel like something is missing . . . more peanut butter! In these bars, peanut butter and chocolate share equal billing. Like the best peanut butter cup, each bite is filled with creamy, sweet, and salty flavors. They are very rich, so cut them into small bars for your bake sale. It's worth it to use top-quality, natural peanut butter without added sugar.

BROWNIE BATTER

- 8 tablespoons (1 stick) unsalted butter
- 4 ounces bittersweet chocolate
- 1 cup granulated sugar
- 2 large eggs
- 1 teaspoon pure vanilla extract
- ½ cup unbleached all-purpose flour
- Pinch of salt

PEANUT BUTTER LAYER

- 1 large egg
- ½ cup granulated sugar
- ¼ cup packed light brown sugar
- ½ teaspoon pure vanilla extract
- ½ cup chunky peanut butter
- ½ cup unbleached all-purpose flour
- ½ teaspoon baking powder
- Pinch of salt
- ⅓ cup chopped roasted, salted peanuts (optional)

1. Preheat the oven to 350°F. Grease a 9" x 9" baking pan with butter or cooking spray. Dust with flour and tap out the excess.

2. *To make the brownie batter:* In a small heavy-bottom saucepan over low heat, warm the butter and chocolate, stirring frequently, until almost completely melted. Remove the saucepan from the heat and stir until smooth. Set aside and cool slightly.

3. In a large bowl, using an electric mixer, beat the sugar, eggs, and vanilla until creamy. Add the cooled chocolate mixture and mix until well combined.

4. Measure the flour and salt and sift directly into the chocolate mixture. Mix until no trace of the dry ingredients remains.

5. Spread a little more than half of the brownie batter evenly in the prepared pan. Put the pan in the refrigerator to chill while you make the peanut butter filling. Reserve the remaining brownie batter.

6. *To make the peanut butter layer:* In a large bowl, using an electric mixer, beat the egg and sugars until light and fluffy. Beat in the vanilla.

7. Using a wooden spoon or a spatula, stir in the peanut butter. Measure the flour, baking powder, and salt and sift directly into the peanut butter mixture. Mix gently until well combined and no trace of the dry ingredients remains.

TIP

If the fund-raiser is for school or children's activities, have the kids handwrite the signs.

peanut butter brownies

8. Remove the pan from the refrigerator and press the peanut butter mixture over the brownie base. (It's easiest to do this with clean fingers. Don't worry about being perfectly even.) Return the pan to the refrigerator for 3 to 5 minutes, until the peanut butter layer firms slightly. Remove the pan from the refrigerator and spread the remaining brownie batter evenly over the top. Toss on the roasted peanuts, if desired.

9. Bake for 35 to 40 minutes, or until a toothpick inserted in the center comes out clean or with only crumbs, not batter, on it. Cool in the pan on a rack for at least 1 hour. Cut into squares just before serving.

Storage: *The brownies will keep longer if they are stored uncut. Cover the pan tightly with plastic wrap or foil and store at room temperature for 3 to 4 days or in the refrigerator for 5 to 7 days.*

cookie crumble

Everyone knows that the best part of a fruit crumble is the crispy topping, so why not make it the star of the show? For this recipe, a big batch of oatmeal cookies is baked and crumbled. Then the crumbs are used as both a crust and a topping. I have to admit, it's a bit involved (and more than a bit messy), but no one will care when they have a shower of cookie crumbs on their shirts and strawberry juice dribbling down their chins. I usually serve a crumble over ice cream. Twice as delicious!

COOKIES

- 6 tablespoons (¾ stick) unsalted butter, room temperature
- ¼ cup packed light brown sugar
- ½ cup granulated sugar
- 1 large egg, room temperature
- 1 tablespoon water
- ½ teaspoon pure vanilla extract
- ½ cup unbleached all-purpose flour
- ¼ teaspoon salt
- ¼ teaspoon baking soda
- 1½ cups quick-cooking oats (not instant)

FILLING

- 3 cups fresh strawberries, washed, dried, and halved
- ¼ cup granulated sugar
- ¼ cup packed light brown sugar
- 2 tablespoons freshly squeezed lemon juice
- 2 tablespoons unsalted butter

1. Preheat the oven to 350°F. Grease 2 baking sheets with butter or line them with parchment paper. Coat a 9" pie plate (use a disposable one if you are preparing the crumble for a bake sale) with butter or cooking spray. Dust with flour and tap out the excess.

2. *To make the cookies:* In a large bowl, using an electric mixer, beat the butter and sugars until light and fluffy. Beat in the egg. Add the water and vanilla and beat to combine.

3. Measure the flour, salt, and baking soda and sift directly into the butter mixture. Beat just until incorporated. Stir in the oats.

4. Drop tablespoons of the dough onto the prepared baking sheets, spacing them at least 1½" apart. (You should have 14 to 18 cookies.) Bake for 15 minutes, or until the edges are set and golden brown and the centers are still soft. Remove the cookies to a rack and cool for at least 1 hour. Leave the oven on.

5. *To make the filling:* While the cookies are cooling, combine the strawberries, sugars, and lemon juice in a large bowl. Toss to combine. Set aside.

6. With your hands, crumble 10 to 12 of the oatmeal cookies and spread them in the bottom of the prepared pie pan. Top with the strawberry mixture. Dice the butter and scatter over the strawberries. Crumble the remaining cookies over the top.

TIP

For a bake sale, I suggest baking crisps and crumbles in disposable pie pans and selling them whole. (Make sure to tell each buyer to eat it the same day or to refrigerate it for up to 2 days before serving.)

7. Bake for 30 to 35 minutes, or until the fruit is soft and bubbly. Cool in the pan on a rack for at least 1 hour. To serve, scoop the crumble into bowls.

Storage: *Cover the crumble with plastic wrap or foil and store in the refrigerator for 1 to 2 days.*

cinnamon toast bars

When I was growing up, Saturday morning was for doing chores: picking up scattered toys, helping to take the trash to the curb, and folding laundry hot from the dryer. My mother would bake these simple, downright cozy bar cookies as our reward. When our rooms were finally clean and everything else was done, we devoured them with big glasses of milk. Every time I bake these treats, my kitchen fills with the scent of cinnamon and I am transported back to my childhood.

The beauty of this recipe is that you probably already have all of the ingredients on hand, making it perfect for that "OMG! I've got to make something for the bake sale!" moment.

Consider slathering Cinnamon Icing (page 175) on top.

---

8 tablespoons (1 stick) unsalted butter, room temperature

1 cup packed light brown sugar

¾ cup granulated sugar

2 large eggs

2 teaspoons pure vanilla extract

1 cup unbleached all-purpose flour

½ teaspoon baking powder

¼ teaspoon salt

2 teaspoons ground cinnamon

1. Preheat the oven to 350°F. Grease a 9" x 9" baking pan with butter or cooking spray. Dust with flour and tap out the excess.

2. In a large bowl, using an electric mixer, beat the butter and sugars until well combined. Then beat in the eggs and vanilla until light and fluffy.

3. Measure the flour, baking powder, salt, and cinnamon and sift directly into the butter mixture. Beat just until combined and no trace of the dry ingredients remains.

4. Spread the batter evenly in the prepared pan and bake for 22 to 28 minutes, or until the top is golden and a toothpick inserted in the center comes out clean or with only crumbs, not batter, on it. Cool in the pan on a rack for 1 hour. Cut into squares just before serving.

Storage: *The bars will keep longer uncut. Cover the pan with plastic wrap or foil and store at room temperature for 3 to 4 days or in the refrigerator for 6 to 8 days.*

chocolate cereal treats

What child has not relished a hard-won, gooey cereal treat after a grueling soccer competition? I'm a big fan of the flavor, but I find most versions far too sticky. Here is my super-simple, no-bake rendition. In place of the marshmallows, I use milk or white chocolate chips and sometimes add chopped nuts. The results are crispy, crunchy, and irresistible. This recipe may not be *quite* as satisfying as scoring the winning goal against the state champs, but it sure is easier!

1. Line a 9" x 9" baking pan with 2 sheets of foil, extending them up the sides.

2. Warm the chocolate chips in a small heavy-bottom saucepan over low heat, stirring constantly, until almost completely melted. Remove the saucepan from the heat and stir until completely smooth. Set aside to cool for 3 to 5 minutes.

3. Pour the cereal into a large mixing bowl. Add the melted chocolate and nuts, if using. Stir with a spatula until well combined.

4. Spread the cereal evenly into the prepared pan and pat down with the spatula. Let stand for at least 30 minutes, or until the mixture is set. Refrigerate for 15 to 30 minutes to set the chocolate. Cut into bars. Serve straight from the refrigerator or at room temperature.

Storage: *Cover the bars with plastic wrap or foil and store at room temperature for 4 to 6 days.*

1½ cups milk or white chocolate chips

3 cups puffed rice cereal, such as Rice Krispies

¼ cup coarsely chopped nuts (optional)

TIP

Location is critical to a bake sale. Consider staging it on the sidelines of a local Little League game or other sporting event.

birthday cake

My mother always baked family birthday cakes from scratch. Just before my 8th birthday, I begged for a store-bought cake with sugared flowers; she gave in and bought a sheet cake from a local bakery. The blue frosting rosettes probably had a longer shelf life than a Twinkie, and I still remember how awful they tasted. Now, whenever I make a white cake, I use her tried-and-true recipe and always frost it with a delicious icing (see Chapter 10).

You don't have to wait for a birthday to bake this cake. Top the frosting with some colorful sprinkles to make any ordinary day worth celebrating!

This recipe makes a single layer, but it is easily multiplied. Double or triple it as you see fit. For a bake sale, you can sell the cake whole, as quarters, or in thick slices.

2 large egg whites

¾ cup granulated sugar, divided

¼ cup vegetable shortening

1¼ cups pastry flour (not self-rising)

1½ teaspoons baking powder

Pinch of salt

½ cup whole milk

½ teaspoon pure vanilla extract

1. Preheat the oven to 350°F. Grease as many 9" round cake pans (or 9" x 9" baking pans) as you plan to have layers with butter or cooking spray, making sure to get the sides. Dust with flour and tap out the excess. Set the pan(s) aside. *Make sure you double or triple the recipe ingredients if you want more than 1 layer.*

2. In a large bowl, using an electric mixer, beat the egg whites until foamy. Gradually add ½ cup of the sugar and beat until soft peaks form. Set aside.

3. Put the vegetable shortening in another large bowl. Measure the flour, baking powder, and salt and sift directly into the shortening. Stir with a wooden spoon until well combined. The mixture will be crumbly. Gradually add the milk, vanilla, and the remaining ¼ cup sugar and stir until well combined.

4. Using a spatula, gently fold in one-third of the egg white mixture until just combined. Then fold in the rest. Be careful not to over-mix. It's okay if there are still some streaks of egg white.

5. Spread the batter into the prepared pan(s). Bake for 30 to 35 minutes, or until a toothpick inserted in the center comes out clean or

with only crumbs, not batter, on it. The center of the cake should spring back when touched lightly. Cool in the pan(s) on a rack for at least 1 hour. Remove from the rack and cool completely on a plate before frosting. If you frost this cake, plan on 2 cups for each layer. You'll be doing the top and sides.

Storage: *To store the frosted cake, stick a few toothpicks into the top and cover with plastic wrap (the toothpicks will keep the frosting from smearing). The cake will keep at room temperature for 3 to 4 days or in the refrigerator for 5 to 7 days.*

cookies and dreams brownies

Fat Witch Bakery is located inside the building where Oreo cookies were invented. How is that for a good omen? These cookie-brownie mash-up treats are a nod to America's favorite sandwich cookie.

12 tablespoons (1½ sticks) unsalted butter

4 ounces bittersweet chocolate, chopped into small, even-size pieces

3 large eggs

1¼ cups granulated sugar

1 teaspoon pure vanilla extract

½ cup + 2 tablespoons unbleached all-purpose flour

Pinch of salt

½ cup white chocolate chips

2 cups slightly crushed Oreo cookies (10–13 cookies)

1. Preheat the oven to 350°F. Grease a 9" x 9" baking pan with butter or cooking spray. Dust with flour and tap out the excess.

2. In a small heavy-bottom saucepan over low heat, warm the butter and bittersweet chocolate, stirring frequently, until almost completely melted. Remove the saucepan from the heat and stir until smooth. Set aside and cool slightly.

3. In a large bowl, using an electric mixer, beat the eggs, sugar, and vanilla until creamy. Add the cooled chocolate mixture and mix until well combined.

4. Measure the flour and salt and sift directly into the chocolate mixture. Mix until no trace of the dry ingredients remains.

5. Spread the batter evenly in the prepared pan and bake for 30 to 35 minutes, or until a toothpick inserted in the center comes out clean. Cool in the pan on a rack for 30 minutes.

6. Warm the white chocolate chips in a small heavy-bottom saucepan over low heat, stirring constantly, until almost completely melted. Remove the saucepan from the heat and stir until completely smooth. (Alternatively, you can melt the chocolate in a microwave oven on medium power in 20- to 30-second bursts.) Using a spatula, spread the white chocolate evenly over the top of the brownies. Immediately scatter the crumbled Oreo cookies over the top. Place the pan in the refrigerator until the topping is firm, at least 30 minutes. Cut into squares just before serving.

Storage: *The brownies will keep longer uncut. Cover the pan with plastic wrap or foil and store at room temperature for 3 to 4 days.*

TIP

Brownies pair with milk! Consider selling shelf-stable cartons of milk.

halfway healthy

I may have built a business on butter, sugar, and chocolate, but I'm a firm believer that sweets can incorporate healthy ingredients, too. Don't worry—I'm not talking about sugar-free desserts devoid of flavor or minuscule portions that wouldn't satisfy your sweet tooth any more than a single drop of milk would satisfy a colicky baby. It's good to give in to your cravings! Just not every single time.

I'll never claim that the treats in this chapter are the pinnacle of nutritious; they are just delicious desserts with a little bit of healthy thrown in. Think tart raspberries, sweet honey, and chewy raisins; brownies lightened with yogurt; cookies studded with heart-healthy macadamia nuts; and breakfast bars packed with nuts and whole grain oats.

If you are planning a better-for-you bake sale, you'll definitely want to include some of these recipes. Even for standard bake sales, it's a smart idea to have one or two whole-some options that will appeal to health-minded customers. Make a special sign so people can spot the more nutritious treats. Decorating the tables with fresh flowers is a way to give a feeling of natural goodness. Just make sure you pick ones that won't shed petals easily. You can also fill mason jars with oats, dried fruits, and pumpkin seeds and place them behind the goodies.

yogurt brownies

Healthy-ish brownies? I was skeptical, too, until I perfected this recipe. Wholesome yogurt and naturally fat-free cocoa powder stand in for more sinful ingredients. I guarantee, no one will miss the old standbys. For the best flavor, use top-quality cocoa powder and full-fat yogurt. At home, I like to serve these with a scoop of vanilla frozen yogurt or raspberry sorbet. For your bake sale, consider selling them in cello bags of two or three. After all, since they are a healthy treat, it's okay to have more than one!

1. Preheat the oven to 350°F. Grease a 9" x 9" baking pan with butter or cooking spray. Dust with flour and tap out the excess.

2. In a large bowl, using an electric mixer, beat the eggs and sugar until frothy and well combined. Beat in the cocoa. Add the yogurt and continue to beat until well combined. Beat in the vanilla and the canola oil.

3. Measure the flour, salt, baking powder, and baking soda and sift directly into the cocoa mixture. Beat just until incorporated and no trace of the dry ingredients remains.

4. Pour the batter into the prepared pan and bake for 35 minutes, or until a toothpick inserted in the center comes out clean or with only moist crumbs, not batter, on it. Cool in the pan on a rack for 1 hour. Cut into squares just before serving.

Storage: *The brownies will keep longer uncut. Cover the pan with plastic wrap or foil and store at room temperature for 3 to 4 days or in the refrigerator for 6 to 8 days.*

2 large eggs

1 cup granulated sugar

¼ cup unsweetened cocoa powder

1 cup full-fat plain yogurt

1 teaspoon pure vanilla extract

¼ cup canola oil

1½ cups unbleached all-purpose flour

½ teaspoon salt

¼ teaspoon baking powder

¼ teaspoon baking soda

Tip

Bake an extra batch, cut them into tiny squares, and skewer each with a toothpick. Offer them up as samples at your bake sale. It's a great way to entice buyers!

pecan bars

Fragrant, crunchy pecans are a bit of a weakness for me. If there is a bowl set out on a bar or coffee table, I have a hard time keeping my hands out of it. I tell myself it's okay, though, because nuts are so healthy. What's one more handful? I'm protecting my heart!

These pecan bars are made with whole wheat flour, and agave syrup and brown rice syrup stand in for most of the sugar. Even though they are a virtuous dessert, they are still quite rich, so cut them into small pieces.

CRUST

- ¾ cup unbleached whole wheat flour
- ¼ cup unbleached all-purpose flour
- 1 teaspoon baking powder
- 1 teaspoon salt
- ⅓ cup packed light brown sugar
- 6 tablespoons (¾ stick) unsalted butter, room temperature
- ¼ cup coarsely chopped pecans

TOPPING

- 3 tablespoons unsalted butter
- ½ cup organic agave syrup
- ⅓ cup brown rice syrup
- 2 teaspoons pure vanilla extract
- ¼ teaspoon salt
- 1 large egg
- 1¾ cups coarsely chopped pecans

Tip These are a wonderful, healthier alternative to traditional pecan pie. Offer them up at any Thanksgiving or fall-themed bake sale.

1. Preheat the oven to 350°F. Grease a 9" x 9" baking pan with butter or cooking spray. Dust with flour and tap out the excess.

2. *To make the crust:* In a large bowl, combine the flours, baking powder, salt, and sugar. Add the butter and beat with a mixer on low speed until well combined and the mixture forms coarse crumbs. Stir in the pecans.

3. With your fingers, press the dough evenly into the bottom of the prepared pan. Bake for 15 minutes, or until the center is golden and the edges are lightly browned. Cool in the pan on a rack. Leave the oven on.

4. *To make the topping:* Melt the butter in a small heavy-bottom saucepan over low heat. Set aside to cool.

5. In a large bowl, combine the agave, brown rice syrup, vanilla, and salt. Add the melted butter and stir until just combined. Add the egg and stir to combine.

6. Pour the mixture over the crust and sprinkle with the pecans. Bake for 20 minutes, or until the filling is barely set at the center (you should see small cracks on the surface). Cool in the pan on a rack for 2 hours. Cut into small squares.

Storage: *Cover the bars with plastic wrap or foil and store at room temperature for 2 to 3 days or in the refrigerator for 5 to 7 days.*

the berry best

Like a lot of people these days, I try to eat locally grown foods, such as vegetables and eggs from nearby farms. But in the depths of winter, when the produce selection is sparse, I can never resist those cartons of raspberries flown in from some far-flung warm place. Forgive me!

I often use them to make these crumbly, oat-filled bars, topped with a thick layer of raspberry jam. The whole raspberries are added after the bars come out of the oven, a trick that highlights their fresh "pop." These are equally good made with any other berry or jam. Sometimes I like to mix things up by combining flavors. Think blueberries with apricot jam or strawberries with cherry jam.

1. Preheat the oven to 350°F. Line a 9" x 9" baking pan with aluminum foil.

2. *To make the crust:* In a large bowl, whisk together the flour, sugar, salt, and baking powder. Stir in the agave and egg. Add the butter and fruit preserves and stir until well combined.

3. Spread the mixture evenly in the bottom of the prepared pan and bake for 15 minutes, or until the edges are a dark amber color. Place the pan on a rack. Leave the oven on.

4. *To make the topping:* In a medium bowl, stir the preserves and oats together. Spread the mixture over the crust, which can be either cool or hot. Return the pan to the oven and bake for an additional 10 minutes, or until the edges are ever-so-slightly bubbly.

5. Quickly nestle the fresh berries into the hot topping. (Don't worry about spacing them evenly. It doesn't have to be perfect!) Cool in the pan on a rack for at least 1½ hours. Remove from the pan by pulling up on the sides of the aluminum foil. Transfer to a plate and place in the refrigerator to chill. Cut into bars before serving.

Storage: *The bars will keep longer uncut. Cover the pan with plastic wrap or foil and store in the refrigerator for 1 to 2 days.*

CRUST

- 1 cup unbleached all-purpose flour
- ¼ cup packed light brown sugar
- 1 teaspoon salt
- ¼ teaspoon baking powder
- ¼ cup organic agave syrup
- 1 large egg
- 6 tablespoons (¾ stick) unsalted butter, room temperature
- 1 tablespoon raspberry preserves

TOPPING

- ¾ cup raspberry preserves
- ⅓ cup quick-cooking oats (not instant)
- 2–3 cups fresh raspberries, rinsed and thoroughly dried

Tip To keep berries beautiful, refrigerate fruit-based treats.

honey-raisin peanut butter bars

There are creamy peanut butter people and there are chunky peanut butter people. I definitely root for team chunky. I love the nubby, crunchy bits and the ever-so-slightly salty bite. In this recipe, I pair my favorite spread with sweet honey and chewy raisins to create a bar packed with energy-boosting power. It's the perfect pre–sports practice or gym session snack. For a bake sale supporting a sports team, they are a must. If you want to sneak in a handful of chocolate chips, I won't tell.

2 large eggs

¾ cup organic cane sugar

½ cup honey

½ cup chunky peanut butter

1 teaspoon pure vanilla extract

2 tablespoons unsalted butter, room temperature

1 cup unbleached all-purpose flour

1 teaspoon baking powder

½ teaspoon salt

½ cup raisins

¼ cup milk chocolate chips (optional)

Tip

List the ingredients of your baked goods, especially if they include allergens.

1. Preheat the oven to 350°F. Grease a 9" x 9" baking pan with butter or cooking spray. Dust with flour and tap out the excess.

2. In a large bowl, using an electric mixer, beat the eggs and sugar until frothy and well combined. Beat in the honey, peanut butter, vanilla, and butter.

3. Measure the flour, baking powder, and salt and sift directly into the peanut butter mixture. Mix gently, just until combined and no trace of the dry ingredients remains. Using a wooden spoon, stir in the raisins and chocolate chips, if using.

4. Spread the batter evenly in the prepared pan. (It may be difficult to spread, but using a spatula will make it easier.) Bake for 25 minutes, or until a toothpick inserted in the center comes out clean or with only moist crumbs, not batter, on it. Cool in the pan on a rack for at least 1 hour. Cut into squares before serving.

Storage: The bars will keep longer uncut. Cover the pan with plastic wrap or foil and store at room temperature for 2 to 3 days or in the refrigerator for 5 to 7 days.

coconut-macadamia nut cookies

Sweet coconut and salty macadamia nuts ensure that these cookies are packed with loads of tropical flavor. The oatmeal adds a healthy fiber boost, so you can feel good about eating them in your bathing suit. These cookies would be perfect for a Hawaiian- or tiki-themed bake sale. I think they are also perfect around Mother's Day, with spring in full bloom and summer just around the corner.

1. Preheat the oven to 350°F. Grease 2 or 3 large baking sheets with butter or cooking spray or line them with parchment paper.

2. In a large bowl, using an electric mixer, beat the butter and sugar until light and fluffy. Beat in the eggs one at a time. Beat in the vanilla.

3. Measure the flour, baking soda, and baking powder and sift directly into the butter mixture. Beat just until combined. Stir in the oats, coconut, and nuts.

4. Using 2 teaspoons, drop balls of dough onto the prepared baking sheet, making sure to space them at least 2" apart. Bake for 12 to 14 minutes, or until the edges are golden and the centers are still soft. Cool on the baking sheets on a rack for 10 minutes. Remove the cookies to the rack and cool completely.

Storage: *The cookies will keep for 3 to 6 days stored in an airtight container at room temperature.*

16 tablespoons (2 sticks) unsalted butter, room temperature

1 cup organic cane sugar

2 large eggs

1 teaspoon pure vanilla extract

1½ cups unbleached all-purpose flour

1 teaspoon baking soda

½ teaspoon baking powder

½ cup quick-cooking oats (not instant)

1 cup shredded, sweetened coconut

1 cup coarsely chopped salted macadamia nuts

Tip Hawaiian-themed parties are popular with all age groups. Get out your loud flowered shirt!

sweet potato brownies

You would have to live under a rock (or perhaps in a cave?) not to have heard of the Paleo Diet, which emphasizes unprocessed and nutrient-rich foods. While I have serious doubts that cavemen and cavewomen foraged cacao beans, pulverized them with their clubs, and made chocolate treats, I'd like to think they would have enjoyed these dense, rich brownies made with sweet potatoes. I like to put these atop a scoop of (non-Paleo) ice cream.

To make the mashed sweet potato, prick 1 large or 2 small sweet potatoes all over with a fork. Wrap with foil and roast in a 400°F oven until soft. Cool the potatoes, then split them open, scoop out the flesh, and mash with a fork.

---

1 cup mashed sweet potato

2 large eggs

½ cup pure maple syrup

1 teaspoon pure vanilla extract

¼ cup refined coconut oil, melted (see melting directions page 94)

⅓ cup unsweetened cocoa powder

¼ teaspoon baking powder

½ teaspoon salt

½ cup almond flour

TIP If you have a freezer and can put someone on an ice-cream-scooping station, it's a scrumptious addition to your bake sale. Brownies, bars, or cookies can be wedged in for a yummy topping.

1. Preheat the oven to 350°F. Grease a 9" x 9" baking pan with coconut oil or cooking spray. Dust with flour and tap out the excess.

2. In a large bowl, using an electric mixer, beat the sweet potato and eggs until smooth. Add the maple syrup, vanilla, and oil and beat until well blended.

3. Measure the cocoa, baking powder, and salt and sift directly into the sweet potato mixture. Stir in the almond flour and mix until combined.

4. Spread the batter evenly in the prepared pan and bake for 32 to 35 minutes, or until a toothpick inserted in the center comes out clean or with only moist crumbs, not batter, on it. Cool in the pan on a rack for at least 1 hour, then transfer to the refrigerator. Cut into squares just before serving.

Storage: *The brownies will keep longer uncut. Cover the pan with plastic wrap or foil and store in the refrigerator for 5 to 7 days.*

snappy ginger cookies

Ginger is good for you. It settles your stomach (think ginger ale) and cleanses your palate (think sushi). It is also warm, spicy, and utterly delicious. Grating fresh ginger is a bit of work, but the results are well worthwhile. If you have a Microplane grater, use it. If not, a box grater will do just fine. To amp up the snappy flavor of these cookies, I top them with chopped crystallized ginger. These are a must at any holiday bake sale.

1. Preheat the oven to 350°F. Grease 2 large baking sheets with butter or cooking spray or line them with parchment paper.

2. In a large bowl, using an electric mixer, cream the butter and sugars until light and fluffy. Beat in the eggs one at a time. Beat in the grated ginger.

3. Measure the flour, ground ginger, baking soda, cinnamon, and salt and sift directly into the butter mixture. Beat just until incorporated.

4. Using 2 teaspoons, drop balls of dough onto the prepared baking sheets, making sure to space them at least 2" apart. Bake for 12 to 14 minutes, or until the cookies are set and golden and cracked on top.

5. When the cookies are just out of the oven, top with the crystallized ginger. Cool on the baking sheets on a rack for 15 minutes. Remove the cookies to the rack and cool completely.

Storage: *The cookies will keep for 3 to 6 days in an airtight container at room temperature.*

12 tablespoons (1½ sticks) unsalted butter, room temperature

½ cup granulated sugar

½ cup packed dark brown sugar

2 large eggs

2 tablespoons freshly grated ginger

2 cups unbleached all-purpose flour

2 teaspoons ground ginger

1 teaspoon baking soda

½ teaspoon ground cinnamon

¼ teaspoon salt

½ cup loosely packed coarsely chopped crystallized ginger

snooze bars

I don't care what you early birds out there say: There is a huge difference between 7:00 a.m., when my alarm goes off, and 7:10, when I actually get up after pounding the snooze button. That said, I'm a bit quicker to throw back the covers if I've baked these bars the night before. Packed with good-for-you ingredients like oats, whole wheat flour, nuts, and seeds, they are one of my absolute favorite breakfasts. They are also great for lunch paired with a container of yogurt. I love dried apricots, but you can use any dried fruit you prefer. If you drizzle the chocolate over the bars when they are hot out of the oven, it will melt in. If you wait until they are cool, it will harden over the surface. Either way, it's delicious.

8 tablespoons (1 stick) unsalted butter

½ cup apple cider (not juice)

1 teaspoon pure vanilla extract

1½ cups quick-cooking oats (not instant)

⅓ cup unbleached all-purpose flour

⅓ cup whole wheat flour

¾ cup packed dark brown sugar

¼ teaspoon salt

¼ cup raw, unsalted pumpkin seeds

¼ cup coarsely chopped cashews

¼ cup coarsely chopped walnuts

½ cup coarsely chopped dried fruit

2 ounces bittersweet chocolate (at least 70% cacao)

Tip Cute bags are a great point-of-sale encouragement to buy.

1. Preheat the oven to 350°F. Grease a 9" x 9" baking pan with butter or cooking spray. Dust with flour and tap out the excess.

2. Melt the butter in a small heavy-bottom saucepan over low heat. Set aside to cool slightly, about 5 minutes. Stir in the apple cider and vanilla.

3. In a large bowl, combine the oats, flours, sugar, and salt. Add the cider mixture and stir until well combined. Stir in the pumpkin seeds, cashews, walnuts, and dried fruit, making sure everything is well combined.

4. With a spatula, spread the batter evenly into the prepared pan. Bake for 30 minutes, or until the edges start to pull away from the sides of the pan and a toothpick inserted in the center comes out with only crumbs, not batter, on it. The top should be brown, slightly cracked, and slightly shiny. Cool in the pan on a rack.

5. Put the chocolate in a small microwaveable bowl and microwave in 20-second bursts until almost completely melted. Remove from the microwave oven and stir until completely melted and smooth. With a fork, drizzle the chocolate over the bars. Cool completely. Cut into bars.

Storage: *Cover the bars with plastic wrap or foil and store at room temperature for 3 to 4 days or in the refrigerator for 6 to 8 days.*

CHAPTER
5

gluten-free goodies

Whether they have a diagnosed allergy or simply feel more energetic without it, lots of people are avoiding gluten these days. I'm all for living a healthy lifestyle, but it's a shame when that means skipping dessert. At least once a week, a customer comes into Fat Witch Bakery hoping to find that perfect, fudgy gluten-free brownie. I truly wish we could oblige, but as I explain every time, it comes down to government health codes. We use wheat flour in our bakery, and even though we clean our equipment so it's spic and span every day, infinitesimally small traces of flour may remain. I feel so terrible watching them leave empty-handed, sweet tooth unsatisfied.

In fact, all those disappointed customers began to haunt me. To think of them never sinking their teeth into a warm chocolate torte or never dunking a freshly baked cookie into a glass of milk! I started to experiment with gluten-free baking at home. After lots of (delicious) trial and error, I finally found those perfect brownies—as well as a whole host of other treats that I've included in this chapter.

Gluten-free baking isn't any more difficult than regular baking. The trick is to find a reliable alternative flour. I like Bob's Red Mill gluten-free flour, which you can buy at most health food stores and well-stocked supermarkets. It's also important to read the labels of all your ingredients. Gluten can sneak in where you least expect it, like in some brands of egg substitutes. Keep in mind that gluten-free doughs and batters need to be refrigerated if not used immediately.

With so many people skipping gluten, offering one or two gluten-free treats at your bake sale is a great idea. Just think about the happy, sugary smiles and grateful thanks you will receive from the child who at last devours a chocolate-studded Pancake Cookie or the mom who is finally able to indulge in a luscious Raspberry-Almond Crumble Bar. Be sure to clearly list the ingredients in all your treats, and you might even want to indicate if something was baked in a kitchen where wheat flour containing gluten is kept.

To all those gluten-free customers out there: I hope you are reading! Finally, you can fulfill your Fat Witch cravings at home.

hazelnut-cream cheese brownies

Cupid must have been perched on my shoulder, watching me crack eggs and melt chocolate, as I developed the recipe for these brownies. I don't know if it's the silky swirls of cream cheese or the crunchy, slightly sweet flavor of the hazelnuts, but there is just something positively romantic about these treats. Of course, they would be a bull's-eye on Valentine's Day, but friends and bake sale shoppers will be head over heels any time of year. Hazelnut flour can be a bit difficult to find. If it's not in stock at your local health food store, order it online.

Usually, I just toss nuts right into the batter. But it's a good idea to toast hazelnuts because it makes removing the skins so much easier and the end result so much tastier. To toast hazelnuts, spread them on a baking sheet and bake in a 400°F oven for 5 to 8 minutes, or until fragrant. Transfer the warm nuts to a clean kitchen towel and rub to remove the skins. Don't worry about getting every last bit. Just do the best you can.

FILLING

- 4 ounces cream cheese, softened to room temperature
- ¼ cup granulated sugar
- 1 large egg white

BROWNIE BATTER

- 4 ounces unsweetened chocolate, chopped into small, even-size pieces
- 8 tablespoons (1 stick) unsalted butter
- 1 cup granulated sugar
- 2 large eggs
- 1 teaspoon pure vanilla extract
- ¾ cup hazelnut flour
- ¼ cup gluten-free baking flour
  Big pinch of salt
- ¼ cup coarsely chopped toasted hazelnuts (skins removed)

1. Preheat the oven to 350°F. Grease a 9" x 9" baking pan with butter and dust with gluten-free flour or use gluten-free cooking spray.

2. *To make the filling:* In a medium bowl, using an electric mixer, beat the cream cheese and sugar until smooth. Add the egg white and beat until well combined. Pour into a pastry or resealable plastic bag and place in the refrigerator while you make the brownie batter.

3. *To make the brownie batter:* In a small heavy-bottom saucepan over low heat, warm the chocolate and butter, stirring frequently, until almost completely melted. Remove the saucepan from the heat and stir until the mixture is smooth. Set aside and cool slightly.

4. In a large bowl, using an electric mixer, beat the sugar, eggs, and vanilla until the mixture is thick and lemony in color. Add the cooled chocolate mixture and beat until smooth. Add the hazelnut flour and mix into the batter until well combined.

5. Measure the gluten-free flour and salt and sift directly into the brownie batter, mixing gently until well combined and no trace of the dry ingredients remains.

6. Using a spatula, spread the brownie batter evenly in the prepared pan. With scissors, snip a small hole off one of the corners of the resealable bag containing the cream cheese mixture. Press on the top of the bag and pipe 12 to 16 big dots on the top of the batter. Dip a butter knife into the pan and gently lift and swirl it through the batter to create a marbled effect. Sprinkle the chopped hazelnuts on top.

7. Bake for 32 to 35 minutes, or until a toothpick inserted in the center comes out clean or with only crumbs, not batter, on it. The cream cheese will be slightly golden. Cool in the pan on a rack for 1 hour. Refrigerate until ready to display at your bake sale. Cut just before serving.

Storage: *These brownies will keep longer uncut. Cover the pan with plastic wrap or foil and store in the refrigerator for 4 to 6 days.*

french Kisses

I used to think meringue was merely a topping for lemon pie. All that changed one Christmas, when I went to visit friends in Paris. After a long day of walking and sightseeing, I stopped in a patisserie filled with the most outrageously fancy pastries. I selected a magnificent bûche de Noël, the traditional French holiday cake shaped like a log and dotted with tiny, perfect meringue mushrooms. In fact, they were so tiny and so perfect that I couldn't help picking off just one and popping it into my mouth. *"C'est si bon!"* Needless to say, by the time I arrived at my friends' apartment, there wasn't a single one left.

These French Kisses are a tribute to those irresistible meringue mushrooms. I promise that these delicate, airy delights will be a *fantastique* addition to your bake sale. If you don't have superfine sugar, you can make your own by pulsing 1 cup granulated sugar in a food processor for 30 seconds. You may need to bake these meringues in batches.

When I make these at home for a dessert, I simply pile them on top of each other. At our bakery, we tuck them into clear cellophane bags and tie them with pretty ribbons.

---

1. Preheat the oven to 250°F. Line 2 large baking sheets with parchment paper.

2. In a large bowl, using an electric mixer, beat the egg whites, vanilla, cream of tartar, and salt until stiff peaks form. Gradually whip in the sugar until the mixture is very stiff and glossy.

3. Using 2 spoons, drop mounds of batter onto the baking sheets, spacing them 2" apart. Twist one spoon to make a tiny curl on top. Bake for 40–45 minutes, or until the kisses are slightly golden. Cool on the baking sheets on a rack for at least 1 hour. Using a metal spatula, gently transfer the kisses to a plate in a single layer (don't stack them until cool). Repeat with the remaining batter, if necessary.

Storage: The meringues will keep for 2 to 3 days stored in an airtight container at room temperature. Do not refrigerate (they will become soggy).

4 large egg whites, room temperature

1 teaspoon pure vanilla extract

¼ teaspoon cream of tartar

Pinch of salt

1¼ cups superfine sugar

TIP

Let buyers know how long baked goods will last.

pancake cookies

It happens to the best of us: You promise to bring cookies to a party and then put off baking them until that afternoon, when you scramble around your kitchen like a crazy person hunting for random dessert-friendly ingredients. A few handfuls of chocolate chips? Score! A glug of vanilla-flavored soy milk? In it goes! On one such occasion, when I couldn't find even a teaspoon of flour in my cupboards, I improvised with a box of gluten-free pancake mix that I found on the shelf. Lo and behold, the cookies were fantastic. If you have a few extra minutes, slather them with a bit of Maple Icing (page 171). I promise, people will *flip* for these Pancake Cookies.

I prefer milk chocolate chips here, but you can use semisweet, too. I like to make large cookies (these are 3" in diameter), so I use soupspoons to scoop the batter. For smaller cookies, use teaspoons and reduce the baking time by a few minutes. Depending on how big you make your cookies, you may need to bake these in batches.

---

1. Preheat the oven to 350°F. Grease 2 large baking sheets with vegetable oil or gluten-free cooking spray or line them with parchment paper.

2. In a large bowl, combine the pancake mix and sugar and stir with a fork until well combined. Add the egg and soy milk and blend thoroughly until no lumps remain and the dough is smooth. Stir in the chocolate chips.

3. Using 2 soupspoons, drop mounds of batter onto the prepared baking sheets, spacing them at least 2" apart. Bake 15 to 18 minutes, or until slightly golden on the edges. Cool on the baking sheet on a rack for at least 10 minutes. Using a metal spatula, remove the cookies to a plate and cool completely.

Storage: *The cookies will keep for 3 to 5 days stored in an airtight container at room temperature.*

1½ cups gluten-free pancake mix
½ cup granulated sugar
1 large egg
½ cup vanilla soy milk
1 cup milk chocolate chips

toffee-chocolate chunks

These Toffee-Chocolate Chunks are impossible to stop eating. There is something about that first crunch that always leads to a grab for seconds—and thirds. When I serve them after a casual dinner party, there are never any leftovers. I've taken to baking a second batch just so guests can have a few to take home. For your bake sale, think about arranging 4 to 6 chunks in a bakery box. People will swoop them up. What's the secret? Rice crackers in place of the usual nuts. They add a fantastic light and airy crunch. You can find plain rice crackers in the Asian food section of most well-stocked supermarkets.

40 gluten-free plain rice crackers, coarsely crumbled

16 tablespoons (2 sticks) unsalted butter

1 cup packed dark brown sugar

1¼ cups semisweet chocolate chips

Tip

Let buyers know if gluten-free treats were baked in a kitchen that has gluten flour.

1. Preheat the oven to 350°F. Line a 9" x 9" baking pan tightly with foil, extending it up the sides. Spread the crumbled rice crackers evenly on the bottom of the pan. Set aside.

2. In a small heavy-bottom saucepan over medium-high heat, bring the butter and sugar to a boil. Reduce the heat to low and simmer, stirring constantly, until the mixture thickens and the sugar is completely dissolved, about 5 minutes.

3. Pour the butter mixture evenly over the rice crackers in the baking pan. Bake for 9 minutes, or until the top is bubbly. Remove the pan from the oven and let sit for 3 to 4 minutes.

4. Sprinkle the chocolate chips evenly over the hot toffee and let stand for 5 minutes, or until melted. Using a spatula, smooth the chocolate into an even layer. Cool in the pan on a rack for 15 minutes, then transfer the pan to the refrigerator and chill until the top is firm, about 1 hour. Remove the pan from the refrigerator and, using the foil as handles, lift the entire bar out of the pan. Break the bar into chunks (no need to be exact).

Storage: *Cover the pan with plastic wrap or foil. Store in the refrigerator and bring to room temperature before serving. The chunks will keep for 3 to 5 days.*

raspberry almond crumble

raspberry-almond crumble bars

These bars are so delicious, you will want to set them front and center at your bake sale. Everyone is sure to be impressed, and no one will guess how simple they are to make—or that they are gluten free! A nutty almond crust is topped with a sweet layer of raspberry filling and a shower of cinnamon-spiked crumbles. Best of all, since they are made with raspberry preserves, you don't have to wait for berry season to bake them. Who couldn't use a little bite of summer in the middle of February?

I turn to this recipe when I need to bake something a whole group will love but there is a gluten-sensitive person in the mix. This is a crowd-pleaser, so don't be surprised if folks who can eat a bagel for breakfast, pizza for lunch, and pasta for dinner love these also.

1. Preheat the oven to 350°F. Grease a 9" x 9" baking pan with butter or gluten-free cooking spray. Dust the bottom and sides with almond flour and tap out the excess.

2. *To make the crust:* In a large bowl, stir the flour and salt together with a fork.

3. In a small bowl, whisk together the oil, agave, and vanilla until smooth. Add to the flour mixture and stir until well combined. The mixture will be crumbly. Press the dough into the bottom of the prepared pan. Bake for 15 minutes, or until the edges are golden brown. Cool in the pan on a rack for 10 to 15 minutes. Leave the oven on.

4. *To make the filling:* When the crust has cooled, spread the preserves evenly over the top.

5. *To make the topping:* In a large bowl, mix the flour, salt, and cinnamon together with a fork.

(continued on page 88)

CRUST

1½ cups almond flour + more for the pan

¼ teaspoon salt

2 tablespoons grapeseed oil

1 tablespoon organic agave syrup

1 tablespoon pure vanilla extract

FILLING

½ cup seedless raspberry preserves (with seeds will work if you cannot find seedless)

TOPPING

1¾ cups almond flour

¼ teaspoon salt

½ teaspoon ground cinnamon

¼ cup grapeseed oil

2 tablespoons organic agave syrup

1 large egg

1 cup sliced almonds

6. In a small bowl, whisk together the oil, agave, and egg until combined. Add to the flour mixture and stir until it forms a crumbly dough. Stir in the sliced almonds. If the mixture is very stiff, you may need to use your hands.

7. Using your fingers, drop big pinches of the topping mixture over the raspberry filling. Press the topping gently into the filling. Bake for 17 to 20 minutes, or until the crumble is slightly browned. Cool in the pan on a rack for at least 1 hour. Cut just before serving.

Storage: *The bars will keep longer uncut. Cover the pan with plastic wrap or foil and store in the refrigerator for 3 to 5 days.*

TIP

Humble containers add charm to your bake sale.

buttermilk brownies

My job requires that I taste-test brownies every day. I know, I know—woe is me! But even though I don't have a full-blown gluten allergy, my stomach lets me know when I've had too much. When that happens, I turn to these sweet, tangy buttermilk brownies to satisfy any chocolate cravings. I promise these will appeal to even the biggest brownie freaks. You might have a tough time convincing people at your bake sale that they are actually gluten free!

---

1. Preheat the oven to 350°F. Grease a 9" x 9" baking pan with butter and dust with gluten-free flour or use gluten-free cooking spray.

2. In a small heavy-bottom saucepan over low heat, warm the chocolate and butter, stirring frequently, until almost completely melted. Remove the saucepan from the heat and stir until the mixture is smooth. Set aside and cool slightly.

3. In a large bowl, using an electric mixer on medium speed, beat the sugar, eggs, buttermilk, and vanilla together for 1 minute. Add the chocolate mixture and blend until smooth.

4. Measure the flour and salt and sift directly into the chocolate mixture. Gently mix the batter until combined and no trace of the dry ingredients remains. Stir in the chocolate chips, if using.

5. Spread the batter evenly in the prepared pan and bake for 25 to 30 minutes, or until a toothpick inserted in the center comes out clean or with only crumbs, not batter, on it. Cool in the pan on a rack for 1 hour. Cut the brownies into squares just before serving.

Storage: *These brownies will keep longer uncut. Cover the pan with plastic wrap or foil and store at room temperature for 2 to 3 days or in the refrigerator for 5 to 7 days.*

4 ounces unsweetened chocolate, chopped into small, even-size pieces

8 tablespoons (1 stick) unsalted butter

1 cup granulated sugar

2 large eggs

3 tablespoons buttermilk

1 teaspoon pure vanilla extract

½ cup gluten-free baking flour

1 teaspoon salt

½ cup semisweet chocolate chips (optional)

chocolate-almond torte

Every bake sale should include family-favorite recipes. This torte is one of mine. I can hear my relatives laughing when they see this—how many birthdays, how many get-togethers? It is delicious and, wonderfully enough, gluten free! For your bake sale, I recommend selling it in quarters. Include a note suggesting that customers cut it into thin slices—it's so dense, rich, and fudgy that a little goes a long way. When serving at home, a dollop of crème fraîche and a small glass of port are wonderful accompaniments and make for a stylish dessert after an elegant meal.

Make sure the almond paste you buy is gluten free.

TORTE

- 1 teaspoon + 8 tablespoons (1 stick) unsalted butter, room temperature, divided
- 1 tablespoon unsweetened cocoa powder
- 4 ounces bittersweet chocolate, chopped into small, even-size pieces
- 3 large eggs, separated
- ½ cup granulated sugar
- ⅓ cup gluten-free almond paste (about 3½ ounces)
- ½ cup gluten-free baking flour
- ¼ teaspoon xanthan gum

GLAZE

- 5 ounces semisweet chocolate, chopped into small, even-size pieces
- 2 tablespoons solid vegetable shortening, such as Crisco
- 3 tablespoons slivered almonds (optional)

1. *To make the torte:* Preheat the oven to 350°F. Grease a 9" round cake pan (or a 9" pie pan) with 1 teaspoon of the butter. Dust with the cocoa and tap out the excess.

2. Warm the bittersweet chocolate in a small heavy-bottom saucepan over low heat, stirring frequently, until almost completely melted. Remove the saucepan from the heat and continue to stir until completely melted. (Alternatively, you can melt the chocolate in a microwave oven on medium power in 30-second bursts.) Set aside to cool for 5 to 10 minutes.

3. In a medium bowl, using an electric mixer, whip the egg whites until soft peaks form. Set aside.

4. In a large bowl, using an electric mixer, cream the sugar and the remaining 8 tablespoons butter until light and fluffy. Beat in the almond paste until smooth. Add the egg yolks one at a time and mix until incorporated, scraping the bowl between additions. Add the cooled chocolate and beat to combine.

5. Measure the flour and xanthan gum and sift directly into the chocolate mixture. Beat until no trace of the flour remains. Carefully fold in the egg whites in 3 additions just until incorporated. Be careful not to overmix.

6. Spread the batter into the prepared pan. Bake for 30 minutes, or until a toothpick inserted in the center comes out clean or with only crumbs, not batter, on it. Be careful not to overbake. Cool in the pan on a rack for 15 minutes, then turn the torte out onto a plate or clean rack and cool completely, at least 1 hour. While the torte cools, prepare the glaze.

7. *To make the glaze:* In a small heavy-bottom saucepan over low heat, warm the semisweet chocolate and shortening, stirring frequently, until almost completely melted. Remove the saucepan from the heat and stir until the mixture is smooth. (Alternatively, you can melt the chocolate and shortening in a microwave oven on medium power in 30-second bursts.) Set aside to cool slightly, stirring frequently.

8. With a spatula, spread the glaze over the top and sides of the torte. Sprinkle the top or edges with the almonds, if using. Let stand until the glaze hardens, at least 1 hour. Refrigerate until ready to serve.

Storage: *Cover the torte with plastic wrap or foil and store in the refrigerator for 3 to 4 days.*

vegan goodies

I bake with butter and eggs every day, but I am also a fan of homemade vegan treats. When I need a dessert to serve or to bring to a party, I turn to the recipes in this chapter as my go-to list.

Oh, yes, I initially thumbed my nose at vegan sweets after tasting the prepackaged ones available from my local supermarket. But I'm someone who knows improvements can be made, so I decided to work on my own versions. I hope you will agree that these are delicious! In fact, we now sell these Vegan Brownies in our Chelsea Market shop (with the disclaimer that we keep butter and eggs on the premises). Consider offering at least one or two clearly marked treats from this chapter at your bake sale. Vegans who might otherwise pass by your display are sure to snap up thick slices of apple loaf cake, brownies, and nutty oatmeal bars. Don't be surprised if you sell to nonvegans, too!

My favorite butter substitute is virgin coconut oil. Coconut oil (tip below) is getting a positive rep these days as a healthy fat. I like the sound of that! You can find it in most health food stores or with other oils in well-stocked supermarkets. After coconut oil, canola oil is my next choice. (Here's a suggestion: Since its mild taste doesn't compete with other flavors, use canola oil to grease baking pans, whether vegan or not.) For an egg replacer, I like Bob's Red Mill brand. It allows me to be precise—you can actually whisk up half an "egg."

If your diet includes only plants, most likely you prefer not to use granulated sugar. (Granulated sugar is not an animal product, but many refineries use animal bone char during processing.) As a replacement, I use vegan cane sugar, maple syrup, brown rice syrup, and agave syrup, all of which can be found in health food stores and well-stocked supermarkets.

Here's to alternative baking with good, sweet tastes!

Coconut oil solidifies below 75°F. To liquefy it, put the jar in a small saucepan of very hot water and let it stand for at least 15 minutes. If it still hasn't melted, set it over low heat and simmer for a few minutes.

big apple loaf

I love to listen to music while I bake. I find nothing more relaxing on a cold winter's night than pouring myself a glass of red wine, putting on some good jazz, and trying out a new recipe. That's just how I came up with this hearty, comforting loaf cake studded with juicy chunks of Granny Smith apples. Because 1920s jazz musicians called New York City the Big Apple, I call this my Big Apple Loaf.

This loaf is a tip of the top hat to all the greats who have played in my city. As Duke Ellington said, "If it sounds good, it is good." I hope this sounds good to you!

To provide a lovely sweet crunch on top of this loaf, I use demerara sugar, which is an unrefined brown sugar with large crystals.

1 small Granny Smith apple, peeled, cored, and finely chopped (about ¾ cup)

2 teaspoons + ½ cup vegan cane sugar

¼ teaspoon + 1 teaspoon ground nutmeg

1 cup unbleached all-purpose flour

¾ cup whole wheat flour

¾ teaspoon baking soda

½ teaspoon ground cinnamon
Pinch of salt

¾ cup unsweetened applesauce

½ cup canola oil

¼ cup organic agave syrup

¼ teaspoon apple cider vinegar

1 tablespoon demerara sugar (optional)

1. Preheat the oven to 325°F. Grease an 8" x 4" loaf pan with canola oil or vegan cooking spray. Dust with flour and tap out the excess.

Tip

Soothing music in the background puts people in the mood to buy.

2. Put the apple pieces in a medium bowl and sprinkle with the 2 teaspoons of cane sugar and ¼ teaspoon nutmeg. Toss to coat.

3. Sift the flours, baking soda, cinnamon, salt, and the remaining nutmeg into a large bowl.

4. In a medium bowl, whisk the applesauce, oil, agave, vinegar, and the remaining cane sugar. Pour the applesauce mixture into the flour mixture and stir until well combined. Stir in the apple chunks.

5. Pour the batter into the prepared pan and sprinkle the demerara sugar (if using) over the top. Bake for 60 to 65 minutes, or until the top and edges are golden brown and a toothpick inserted in the center comes out clean or with only crumbs, not batter, on it. Cool completely in the pan on a rack for at least 1 hour.

Storage: *Cover the cake with plastic wrap or foil and store at room temperature for 2 to 4 days or in the refrigerator for 5 to 7 days.*

FAT WITCH BAKE SALE

orange-pine nut cookies

These cookies strike the perfect balance between tartness and sweetness. Orange peel, juice, and marmalade ensure they pack a serious citrusy zing, while pine nuts impart a delicate, buttery crunch.

Toasting nuts usually isn't necessary, but when it comes to pine nuts, it really brings out their flavor. To toast the pine nuts, spread them on a baking sheet and bake in a 350°F oven for 5 to 10 minutes. Watch them carefully, as they are quick to burn.

1. Preheat the oven to 350°F. Grease 2 baking sheets with canola oil or vegan cooking spray or line them with parchment paper.

2. Sift the flours, sugar, baking powder, baking soda, and salt into a large bowl. Add the oil, orange peel, orange juice, and applesauce and mix until well combined. Using your hands, knead the mixture until it comes together into a dough.

3. Scoop up a tablespoon of the dough and roll it into a ball. Place it on one of the prepared baking sheets and, with a damp thumb, make an indentation. Spoon about ¼ teaspoon marmalade into the indentation. Press 6 to 8 pine nuts on top of the marmalade. Repeat with the remaining dough, space the balls at least 1" apart.

4. Bake the cookies for 15 to 18 minutes, or until they are golden and crisp at the edges and still soft in the center. Transfer the cookies to a rack and cool for 1 hour.

Storage: The cookies will keep for 5 to 7 days stored in an airtight container at room temperature.

1 cup unbleached all-purpose flour

½ cup coconut flour

¼ cup vegan cane sugar

¼ teaspoon baking powder

¼ teaspoon baking soda

Pinch of salt

¼ cup virgin coconut oil, melted (see page 94)

3 tablespoons freshly grated orange peel (from 1–2 oranges)

½ cup freshly squeezed orange juice

¼ cup organic applesauce

¼ cup orange marmalade

¼ cup toasted pine nuts

Tip Sell cookies with mugs of herbal tea at your bake sale.

graham cracker squares

I promise, once you bake these, you will never again reach for that box of supermarket graham crackers. Sweet and crisp, these are layered with the wholesome flavors of maple syrup, cinnamon, and nutty graham flour. Use them as a base for all kinds of treats. I like to slather them with almond butter or jam or dip them in pudding.

For this recipe, you will need to use a vegan butter substitute. I like Earth Balance.

½ cup vegan butter substitute
½ cup organic agave syrup
¼ cup pure maple syrup
1¾ cups whole wheat flour
½ cup graham flour
1 teaspoon salt
1 teaspoon baking soda
1 teaspoon ground cinnamon

Tip

Sell a concept. Pair these graham crackers with vegan marshmallows and chocolate.

1. Line two 18" x 12" sheet pans with parchment paper.

2. In a large bowl, using an electric mixer, beat the butter substitute, agave, and maple syrup until well combined and light in color.

3. Measure the flours, salt, baking soda, and cinnamon and sift directly into the bowl. Beat until well combined.

4. Divide the dough in half and shape each half into a flat round. Wrap in plastic wrap and refrigerate until well chilled, about 3 hours.

5. Preheat the oven to 350°F.

6. Remove 1 chilled dough round from the refrigerator and unwrap. Using a rolling pin, roll out the dough on a lightly floured surface. It should measure 9" x 15" and be about ⅛" thick.

7. With a sharp knife or pizza cutter, cut the dough into 12 to 14 squares (3" x 3" each). Using a metal spatula, transfer the squares to one of the prepared baking sheets. With a fork, poke each cracker 3 times in a row down the center. Repeat with the second dough round.

8. Bake for 20 to 24 minutes, or until lightly browned. Cool on the baking sheets on a rack for at least 15 minutes. Remove the crackers to a flat platter and cool completely, at least 1 hour.

Storage: *The crackers will keep for 7 days stored in an airtight container at room temperature.*

vegan brownies

Don't be fooled by the short list of simple ingredients. These brownies are anything but ho-hum! In fact, even if you are not a vegan, this just might become your go-to recipe—especially if you like thick, slightly cakey brownies reminiscent of school lunch-box treats. I sometimes toss in ½ cup coarsely chopped walnuts. These are so good, we sell them at our Chelsea Market shop with the disclaimer that we do keep butter and eggs on the production premises.

1. Preheat the oven to 350°F. Grease a 9" x 9" baking pan with canola oil or vegan cooking spray. Dust with flour and tap out the excess.

2. Sift the flour, sugar, cocoa, baking powder, and salt into a large bowl. Add the water and oil and stir to combine. Stir in the vanilla. Stir in the walnuts, if using.

3. Spread the batter into the prepared pan. Bake for 30 to 35 minutes, or until a toothpick inserted in the center comes out clean or with only moist crumbs, not batter, on it. Cool in the pan on a rack for 1 hour. Cut into shapes just before serving.

Storage: *The brownies will keep longer uncut. Cover the pan with plastic wrap or foil and store at room temperature for 4 to 5 days or in the refrigerator for 6 to 8 days.*

1½ cups unbleached
    all-purpose flour
1½ cups vegan cane sugar
½ cup unsweetened
    cocoa powder
½ teaspoon baking powder
1 teaspoon salt
¾ cup water
¾ cup canola oil
1 teaspoon pure vanilla extract
½ cup chopped walnuts
    (optional)

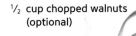

TIP

Brownies don't always have to be square! Use cookie cutters to make different shapes.

go to seed bars

Store-bought energy bars are great for a boost, but half the ingredients are things I've never heard of! That's why I created these homemade power bars, loaded with great-for-you oats, nuts, and seeds. They are chocolate free, but I promise you won't miss it. If you can't find flaxseeds, just increase the amount of the other seeds a bit. You can use any nut you prefer in place of the walnuts.

To toast the sesame seeds, spread them on a baking sheet and bake at 350°F for 6 to 8 minutes.

These bars are an obvious choice for your next hiking trip, but they are also surprisingly pretty. Be sure to display them front and center at your bake sale.

¼ cup organic agave syrup

¾ cup unsweetened organic applesauce

1½ cups organic old-fashioned rolled oats

¼ cup golden flaxseeds (not ground)

⅓ cup chopped walnuts

⅓ cup roasted, unsalted sunflower seeds

⅓ cup toasted sesame seeds

2 tablespoons unsalted pumpkin seeds

Pinch of salt

¾ cup chopped dried fruit (such as apricots, pineapple, and cherries)

1. Preheat the oven to 350°F. Grease a 9" x 9" baking pan with canola oil or vegan cooking spray.

2. Put the agave in a large microwaveable bowl and microwave on medium power for 15 seconds. Remove the bowl from the microwave oven and stir in the applesauce, oats, flaxseeds, walnuts, sunflower seeds, sesame seeds, pumpkin seeds, and salt. Add the dried fruit and stir to combine.

3. Spread the mixture into the prepared pan and smooth the top with a spatula. Bake for 20 minutes, or until set but slightly soft to the touch. Cool in the pan on a rack for 1 hour. Cut into bars.

Storage: Cover the bars with plastic wrap or foil and store at room temperature for up to 5 days.

black and white cookies

From bagels with lox and giant slices of pizza to street-cart pretzels and hot dogs, New York is home to many legendary foods. One of the city's most famous sweets is the black and white cookie, composed of a cakey base roughly the size of a teacup saucer slathered half with vanilla and half with chocolate frosting. My vegan friend Doug confessed they were what he missed most since he'd changed his diet. I was determined to satisfy his craving, so I set out to develop a vegan version. After a lot of (delicious) trial and error, I perfected my recipe. Doug is eternally grateful, and you would never guess these are practically healthy!

COOKIES

- 2 cups plain unsweetened almond milk
- 1 tablespoon + 1 teaspoon apple cider vinegar
- 3¼ cups unbleached all-purpose flour
- 6 tablespoons coconut flour
- ½ teaspoon baking powder
- ¼ teaspoon baking soda
- ¾ cup + 1 tablespoon canola oil
- 1¾ cups vegan cane sugar
- 1 teaspoon salt
- ¼ teaspoon pure vanilla extract
- ¼ teaspoon lemon extract

VANILLA ICING

- 3 tablespoons organic agave syrup
- 4 tablespoons water
- 3½ cups organic confectioners' sugar
- ½ teaspoon pure vanilla extract

CHOCOLATE ICING

- 2 ounces unsweetened chocolate
- 6 tablespoons organic agave syrup
- 4 tablespoons water
- 3½ cups organic confectioners' sugar
- ½ teaspoon pure vanilla extract

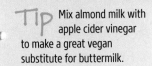

Tip Mix almond milk with apple cider vinegar to make a great vegan substitute for buttermilk.

1. Preheat the oven to 375°F. Line 2 large baking sheets with parchment paper.

2. *To make the cookies:* In a small bowl, whisk together the almond milk and vinegar and let stand for a few minutes. The liquids should separate and look curdled. (Don't worry, this is supposed to happen.)

3. Meanwhile, in a large bowl, sift the flours, baking powder, and baking soda.

4. In another bowl, whisk together the oil, sugar, salt, vanilla, and lemon extract. Add the almond milk mixture and stir to combine. Pour into the flour mixture and whisk until fully combined and smooth.

5. Using a ¼-cup measure, drop scoops of batter onto the prepared baking sheets, making sure to space them at least 2" apart (you should have about 8 cookies per baking sheet). Bake for 20 minutes, or until the cookies are puffed and the edges are golden brown. Cool on the baking sheets on a rack for 5 minutes. Remove the cookies to the rack and cool completely. Repeat with the remaining batter.

6. *To make the vanilla icing:* In a small heavy-bottom saucepan, combine the agave and water and bring to a boil. Immediately remove the saucepan from the heat and whisk in the sugar and vanilla until smooth.

7. Hold one cookie at an angle over the saucepan and, using a large spoon, carefully drip the vanilla icing over half of the flat (bottom) surface. Repeat with the remaining cookies. Return the cookies to the rack while you make the chocolate icing.

8. *To make the chocolate icing:* Put the chocolate in a microwaveable bowl and microwave on medium power, stirring every 30 seconds, until almost completely melted. Remove the bowl from the microwave and stir until completely melted and smooth.

9. In a small heavy-bottom saucepan, combine the agave and water and bring to a boil. Immediately remove the saucepan from the heat and whisk in the melted chocolate. Whisk in the sugar and vanilla until smooth.

10. Hold one cookie at a time at an angle over the saucepan and carefully drip the chocolate frosting over the second half of it. Allow the chocolate to overlap the vanilla iced half ever so slightly so that the entire cookie is completely frosted. If the chocolate icing becomes too stiff, heat it gently in the microwave in 15-second bursts.

11. Let the cookies stand on the rack until the icing has set, at least 30 minutes.

Storage: *These cookies will keep for 4 to 6 days stored in an airtight container at room temperature. Do not stack these cookies.*

maple-pumpkin-oatmeal bars

makes 12 to 16 bars

I love the fall for its crisp, cool air, brilliantly hued leaves, and the pyramid displays of canned pumpkin at the supermarket. Those cans make baking with this delicious winter squash a breeze. These bars are the perfect autumn treat and a must for any back-to-school bake sale. I always tuck one in my backpack before a hike (or in the glove compartment before a scenic drive!). Use real maple syrup—imitation flavor just won't do. Be sure to buy plain canned pumpkin and not pumpkin pie filling, which has added sugar and spices.

1. Preheat the oven to 350°F. Grease a 9" x 9" baking pan with canola oil or vegan cooking spray. Dust with flour and tap out the excess.

2. In a medium bowl, combine the maple syrup and pecans and toss to combine. Set aside for 10 minutes. Stir in the oil, pumpkin, and vanilla.

3. In a large bowl, stir together the flour, oats, and salt with a fork. Add the pumpkin mixture and stir with a wooden spoon or spatula until well blended.

4. Using a spatula or clean hands, spread the dough evenly into the prepared pan and bake for 35 minutes, or until the top is golden brown and the edges are starting to pull away from the sides of the pan. Cool in the pan on a rack for 1 hour. Cut into bars.

Storage: *Cover the bars with plastic wrap or foil and store at room temperature for 7 days.*

½ cup pure maple syrup
1 cup pecans, coarsely chopped
½ cup virgin coconut oil, melted (see page 94)
1 cup canned pumpkin puree
1 teaspoon pure vanilla extract
1 cup unbleached all-purpose flour
1½ cups quick-cooking oats (not instant)
1 teaspoon salt

Tip

The simplest baked goods look elegant on cake stands.

The unexpected

Baking is a meticulous form of cooking, filled with precise measurements and temperatures and specific orders of ingredients. That being said, you might be surprised to learn that I love to change up dessert recipes. I may follow the rules when it comes to fire codes and traffic laws, and I always read the fine print on medicine bottles, but in the Fat Witch kitchen, I release my inner rebel. Years of professional experience have taught me that while baking might be exacting, there is also plenty of room for experimentation.

The recipes in this chapter range from elegant apricot-almond bars scented with fresh rosemary to blondies loaded with peanuts and pretzels. Yet they all have one thing in common: Each incorporates an element of surprise—be it a pop of sea salt, a bite of smoky bacon, a splash of grapefruit juice, or a healthy dose of chocolate where you least expect it. (Hint: This isn't your grandmother's fruitcake.)

Some of these desserts were invented with a specific idea in mind, such as to create the ultimate spicy brownie or to develop my own version of fig bars using the best-quality jam and fresh fruit. Others were simply happy accidents or recipes I developed on a whim when I decided to bake something using the hodgepodge contents of my refrigerator and freezer. I encourage you to read through this chapter with an open mind. Feel free to make substitutions and try out new flavor combinations. Have fun and don't be afraid to go a little crazy. There's no telling how delicious the end results will be.

These treats are sure to keep your bake sale customers intrigued—and coming back for more!

sweet-and-salty caramel blondies

makes 12 to 16 blondies

Tender, buttery blondies are delectable on their own. However, add a little crunch, a little salt, and a little caramel and the results are mouthwatering. Look no further than this recipe for an upgrade to supremely scrumptious. A golden blondie base is topped with honey, peanuts, and crushed pretzels for a perfect union of gooey, salty, and sweet. The peanuts and chunks of pretzels make for a dramatic presentation, so these are always bake sale bestsellers—be sure they are in an easy-to-grab place on the table. Of course, a little chocolate never hurt anything, so I usually drizzle some over the top.

BLONDIES

- 10 tablespoons (1¼ sticks) unsalted butter
- 1½ cups packed light brown sugar
- 2 large eggs, room temperature
- 1 teaspoon pure vanilla extract
- 1 cup unbleached all-purpose flour
- 1½ teaspoons baking powder
- 1 teaspoon salt

TOPPING

- 1 cup granulated sugar
- ½ cup water
- ½ cup honey
- 4 tablespoons (½ stick) unsalted butter
- ¼ cup sweetened condensed milk
- 2½ cups roasted skinned peanuts
- 1½ cups thin pretzel twists, coarsely chopped
- 1 tablespoon coarse sea salt
- 1 cup semisweet chocolate chunks or chips (optional)

1. Preheat the oven to 350°F. Grease a 9" x 9" baking pan with butter or cooking spray. Dust with flour and tap out the excess.

2. *To make the blondies:* Melt the butter in a small heavy-bottom saucepan over low heat, stirring frequently. Pour the melted butter into a large mixing bowl, add the sugar, and stir until well combined. Beat in the eggs one at a time. Beat in the vanilla.

3. Measure the flour, baking powder, and salt and sift directly into the butter mixture. Mix until well combined. Pour the batter into the prepared pan and bake for 20 to 25 minutes, or until a toothpick inserted in the center comes out clean or with only moist crumbs, not batter, on it. Cool in the pan on a rack for at least 1 hour.

4. *To make the topping:* In a medium heavy-bottom saucepan over low heat, combine the sugar and water and stir until the sugar dissolves. Increase the heat and boil without stirring for 10 to 12 minutes, until the mixture is amber colored. Add the honey and return to a boil, stirring for about 1 minute. Add the butter and stir until melted and well combined. Whisk in the condensed milk, then stir in the peanuts. Pour the topping over the cooled blondies. Sprinkle with the crushed pretzels and salt.

5. Put the chocolate chunks or chips, if using, in a microwaveable bowl and microwave on medium power, stirring every 45 seconds,

TIP

Individual containers are a pretty way to display sweets and make them easier to transport.

until the chocolate is almost completely melted. Remove the bowl from the microwave oven and stir until completely smooth. Using a fork, drizzle the chocolate over the blondies.

6. Chill the blondies in the refrigerator for at least 30 minutes. Cut into squares. Serve at room temperature.

Storage: *The blondies will keep longer uncut. Cover the pan with plastic wrap or foil and store at room temperature for 2 to 3 days.*

fig manhattans

No offense to Newton, Massachusetts, but I've always found a certain fig-filled cookie does not give figs the attention they deserve. It's such a shame, because plump, juicy figs are luscious in their own right. I decided it was high time to show them off Manhattan-style. These bars are chic and sophisticated (dare I say sexy?). I use high-quality fig jam, as it's easier than boiling down tons of fresh figs. A layer of sliced figs on top will keep them looking fresh and fabulous. Fresh figs are in season only in summer. These bars are a must for any warm weather bake sale but not for outdoors. Keep refrigerated.

1. Preheat the oven to 350°F. Grease a 9" x 9" baking pan with butter or cooking spray. Line the bottom with parchment paper. Dust with flour and tap out the excess.

2. *To make the crust:* In a large bowl, using an electric mixer, cream the butter and sugar until light and fluffy. Add the egg and egg yolk and beat to combine. Beat in the vanilla.

3. Measure the flour and salt and sift directly into the butter mixture. Gently stir in the jam.

4. With a spatula, spread the batter evenly into the prepared pan. Bake for 30 minutes, or until lightly golden brown. Cool in the pan on a rack. Leave the oven on. While the crust is cooling, prepare the topping.

5. *To make the topping:* In a large bowl, whisk the jam, apple cider, honey, and cinnamon until well blended. Pour over the crust and bake for 20 minutes, or until the topping is bubbling and the edges are set. Leave the oven on.

(continued on page 118)

CRUST

12 tablespoons (1½ sticks) unsalted butter, room temperature

⅓ cup granulated sugar

1 large egg + 1 large egg yolk

1 teaspoon pure vanilla extract

1¾ cups unbleached all-purpose flour

¼ teaspoon salt

2 tablespoons fig jam

TOPPING

1½ cups fig jam

¼ cup apple cider

2 tablespoons honey

1 teaspoon ground cinnamon

2 pints fresh figs, washed and dried

3 tablespoons sugar

6. Cut the figs into quarters and arrange them evenly over the topping. Sprinkle with the sugar. Return the pan to the oven for 5 minutes, or until the figs have softened slightly and the sugar is caramelized. Cool in the pan on a rack for at least 1 hour. Cut into squares just before serving.

Storage: *The bars will keep longer uncut. Cover the pan with plastic wrap or foil and store in the refrigerator for 2 to 4 days.*

TIP

Make a card suggesting serving treats with a dollop of soft goat cheese or tiny slather of crème fraîche.

bacon brownies

Bacon desserts have been blogged about, bragged about, and raved about. If you're late to the party and haven't yet tried a porkified sweet treat, let me tell you—they taste *good*. There is just something magical about the combination of sweet sugar and smoky, salty bacon. After much experimentation, here is my recipe for brownies doctored up with everyone's favorite breakfast meat. A guaranteed crowd-pleaser, it goes without saying that these brownies pair perfectly with your morning cup of joe.

1. Preheat the oven to 350°F. Grease a 9" x 9" baking pan with butter or cooking spray. Dust with flour and tap out the excess.

2. In a large skillet, fry the bacon strips until crisp. Transfer the bacon to paper towels to drain and dry. (Change the paper towels once to get rid of some of the grease.) Crumble the bacon into a small bowl and add the cocoa. Toss to combine and set aside.

3. In a small heavy-bottom saucepan over low heat, warm the butter and chocolate, stirring frequently, until almost completely melted. Remove the saucepan from the heat and stir until smooth. Set aside and cool slightly.

4. In a large bowl, using an electric mixer, beat the sugar, eggs, and vanilla until creamy. Add the cooled chocolate mixture and mix until well combined.

5. Measure the flour and salt and sift directly into the chocolate mixture. Mix until no trace of the dry ingredients remains. Stir in the cocoa-covered bacon.

6. Spread the batter evenly in the prepared pan and bake for 30 to 35 minutes, or until a toothpick inserted in the center comes out clean or with only moist crumbs, not batter, on it. Cool in the pan on a rack for 1 hour. Cut the brownies into squares just before serving.

Storage: *The brownies will keep longer uncut. Cover the pan with plastic wrap or foil and store in the refrigerator for 5 to 7 days.*

8–12	strips bacon
3	tablespoons unsweetened cocoa powder
12	tablespoons (1½ sticks) unsalted butter
4	ounces bittersweet chocolate (at least 60% cacao), chopped into small, even-size pieces
1¼	cups granulated sugar
3	large eggs, room temperature
1	teaspoon pure vanilla extract
½	cup + 2 tablespoons unbleached all-purpose flour
	Pinch of salt

Tip

Set up a "breakfast treats" area at your bake sale featuring these brownies, Snooze Bars (page 72), and Pancake Cookies (page 83).

apricot–almond–rosemary bars

If you're anything like me, you have an odd assortment of ingredients in your kitchen. I can't remember what I intended the almond butter for, or why I had fresh rosemary wrapped in plastic in the freezer or dried apricots tucked in the back of a cabinet.

One bitterly cold January afternoon, my need for something warm and sweet became overwhelming. The icy snow falling in Manhattan made running to the store for ingredients impossible. So I opened the cabinet doors and peeked inside my freezer.

What follows is the dessert I came up with. Since that winter, I've baked it whenever I want something ever-so-slightly different.

CRUST

- 1 cup unbleached all-purpose flour
- 1 teaspoon salt
- ¼ teaspoon baking powder
- ¼ cup granulated sugar
- ¼ cup packed light brown sugar
- 1 large egg, room temperature
- 4 tablespoons (½ stick) unsalted butter, room temperature
- 2 tablespoons almond butter, room temperature

TOPPING

- 3 tablespoons unsalted butter, room temperature
- 1 tablespoon almond butter, room temperature
- ⅓ cup granulated sugar
- 1 pound dried apricots, sliced in half
- 2 teaspoons chopped fresh rosemary

1. Preheat the oven to 350°F. Grease a 9" x 9" baking pan with butter or cooking spray. Line the bottom with parchment paper. Dust with flour and tap out the excess.

2. *To make the crust:* In a large bowl, sift together the flour, salt, and baking powder. Add the sugars and stir to combine. Add the egg, butter, and almond butter and, using a large fork or clean hands, mix until well incorporated.

3. Using your fingers, spread the dough evenly in the prepared pan. Bake for 15 to 18 minutes, or until the crust is light golden brown and bounces back a little when pressed. Cool in the pan on a rack for 5 to 10 minutes. Leave the oven on.

4. *To make the topping:* In a large bowl, using an electric mixer, beat the butter and almond butter together. Add the sugar and mix until well combined.

TIP

Putting your treats in baskets is the perfect homey touch.

5. When the crust has cooled, arrange the apricots evenly over the top. Don't worry about making it look perfect! Using your fingers, drop pinches of the topping mixture evenly over the apricots. Return the pan to the oven and bake for 18 to 20 minutes, or until the topping is golden brown. Sprinkle with the rosemary. Cool in the pan on a rack for at least 1 hour. Cut into bars.

Storage: *The bars will keep longer uncut. Cover the pan with plastic wrap or foil and store in the refrigerator for 3 to 6 days.*

fruitcake brownies

This is not your grandmother's fruitcake recipe. Instead of a soggy, leaden cake, relegated to the back of the dessert table, this is a rich brownie infused with just the right amount of boozy fruit. I promise it won't be regifted. Fruitcake is traditionally made with brandy, but I substitute rum for an unexpected twist. Use whichever you prefer. You can also soak the dried fruit for longer than 24 hours for a more pronounced alcohol flavor. After draining the soaked fruit, you can either discard the rum or savor the few delicious sips while the brownies are in the oven.

I usually drizzle Buttercream Perfection (page 169) on top. If you are so inclined, you can add a few drops of rum when mixing the icing.

---

2 cups coarsely chopped dried fruit, such as apricots, golden raisins, cherries, or prunes

1 cup dark rum

10 tablespoons (1¼ sticks) unsalted butter

4 ounces unsweetened chocolate, chopped into small, even-size pieces

3 large eggs

1 cup granulated sugar

1 teaspoon pure vanilla extract

1 cup unbleached all-purpose flour

Pinch of salt

1. At least 24 hours before you plan to bake the brownies, combine the dried fruit and rum in a large bowl. Make sure there is at least 2" of room in the bowl above the fruit-rum mixture. (This allows some of the alcohol to evaporate and prevents the fruit from becoming soggy.) Cover the bowl with plastic wrap. Set aside in a cool, dry place, away from any heat source.

2. When you are ready to bake the brownies, drain the fruit in a colander for 30 minutes.

3. Preheat the oven to 350°F. Grease a 9" x 9" baking pan with butter or cooking spray. Dust with flour and tap out the excess.

4. In a small heavy-bottom saucepan over low heat, warm the butter and chocolate, stirring frequently, until almost completely melted. Remove the saucepan from the heat and stir until smooth. Set aside and cool slightly.

5. In a large bowl, using an electric mixer, beat the eggs and sugar until creamy. Beat in the vanilla and then the cooled chocolate mixture.

TIP

A funny sign brings a little warmth and humor to your bake sale.

6. Measure the flour and salt and sift directly into the batter. Beat just until no trace of the dry ingredients remains. Stir in the dried fruit.

7. Spread the batter evenly in the prepared pan. Bake for 30 to 35 minutes, or until a toothpick inserted in the center comes out clean or with only crumbs, not batter, on it. Cool in the pan on a rack for at least 1 hour. Cut just before serving.

Storage: *The brownies will keep longer uncut. Cover the pan with plastic wrap or foil and store at room temperature for 2 to 3 days or in the refrigerator for 5 to 7 days.*

lemon-grapefruit bars

Tart Ruby Red grapefruit doesn't have to be relegated only to the breakfast table or juice glass! I think it has been long overlooked as a baking ingredient. In this recipe, I give standard lemon bars an unexpected, slightly sour twist with fresh-squeezed grapefruit juice and zippy pomegranate seeds, which pair perfectly with the buttery shortbread crust. I find lemons much easier to work with, but use grapefruit peel in place of the lemon peel, if you like. These bars are sure to stand out at any bake sale—and make kids' lips pucker.

1. Preheat the oven to 350°F. Grease a 9" x 9" baking pan with butter or cooking spray. Line the bottom with parchment paper. Dust with flour and tap out the excess.

2. *To make the crust:* In a large bowl, sift the flour, sugar, and salt. Using a big fork or your clean fingers, work the butter into the flour mixture until it is well combined. Pat the mixture evenly into the bottom of the prepared pan and bake for 15 to 18 minutes, or until lightly golden brown. Cool in the pan on a rack. Leave the oven on.

3. *To make the filling:* Put the eggs in a medium bowl and beat with an electric mixer until frothy. Slowly add the sugar and beat just until combined. Beat in the lemon and grapefruit juices and the lemon peel.

4. Measure the flour and salt and sift directly into the juice mixture. Stir gently, just until incorporated. Pour the mixture over the baked crust and sprinkle with the pomegranate seeds, if using. (They will stay suspended beautifully near the top as they bake.)

5. Bake for 18 to 22 minutes, or until the filling is set. It should have tiny bubbles on the surface and the edges will be very slightly brown. Cool in the pan on a rack for at least 1 hour.

Storage: *The bars will keep longer uncut. Cover the pan with plastic wrap or foil and store in the refrigerator for 3 to 5 days.*

CRUST

- 1 cup unbleached all-purpose flour
- ½ cup confectioners' sugar
- ½ teaspoon salt
- 8 tablespoons (1 stick) unsalted butter, room temperature

FILLING

- 3 large eggs
- 1 cup granulated sugar
- 1 cup freshly squeezed lemon juice (3–4 lemons)
- ¼ cup freshly squeezed Ruby Red grapefruit juice (½ grapefruit)
- 1½ tablespoons fresh, finely grated lemon peel (1–2 lemons)
- 3 tablespoons unbleached all-purpose flour
- Big pinch of salt
- ½ cup fresh pomegranate seeds (optional)

cayenne-coffee brownies

Ancient Aztec kings drank massive amounts of hot chocolate each day—only instead of sweetening it with sugar, they added zesty spices. These cocoa brownies are not for the faint of heart—or palate! A healthy dose of cayenne pepper ensures they pack a hot hit of fire. The coffee pairs beautifully with the chocolate. Make sure you warn customers at your bake sale.

I like to frost these brownies with Coffee-Caramel Icing (page 172) as an interesting balance to the peppery punch.

---

12 tablespoons (1½ sticks) unsalted butter

½ cup unsweetened cocoa powder

1½ cups granulated sugar

3 large eggs

1 tablespoon pure vanilla extract

2 tablespoons instant coffee granules mixed with 1½ teaspoons hot water

¾ cup unbleached all-purpose flour

½ teaspoon salt

½ teaspoon cayenne pepper

⅓ cup milk chocolate chips

Tip

Consider a table of treats that don't fall into any of the "usual" categories.

1. Preheat the oven to 350°F. Grease a 9" x 9" baking pan with butter or cooking spray. Dust with flour and tap out the excess.

2. Heat the butter in a small heavy-bottom saucepan over low heat, stirring occasionally, until just melted (be careful not to let it brown). Set aside to cool.

3. Sift the cocoa into a large bowl. Add the sugar and melted butter and whisk until blended. Add the eggs, one at a time, whisking until the mixture is smooth and shiny. Stir in the vanilla and coffee mixture.

4. Measure the flour and salt and sift directly into the cocoa mixture. Stir gently, just until combined. Stir in the cayenne. Fold in the chocolate chips.

5. Spread the batter evenly in the prepared pan and bake for 30 to 35 minutes, or until a toothpick inserted in the center comes out clean or with only moist crumbs, not batter, on it. Cool in the pan on a rack for at least 1 hour. Cut into squares before serving.

Storage: The brownies will keep longer uncut. Cover the pan with plastic wrap or foil and store at room temperature for 3 to 5 days or in the refrigerator for 6 to 8 days.

foreign accents

One of the things I love about America is the diversity of its culinary traditions. This is especially true of New York City, where not only can you find the best Chinese soup dumplings, Jewish bagels, and Korean *bibimbap,* you can have them delivered right to your door at 3:00 a.m. But walk through any supermarket in the country these days and you are sure to find a wealth of international ingredients, from Indian spices to Swiss chocolate, Italian espresso, and Greek phyllo dough.

This chapter is a salute to everyone who landed at Ellis Island with satchels, steamer trunks, valises, and suitcases in hand. Tucked inside their possessions were pastry recipes from home. I've done my best to incorporate some of my favorite foreign flavors into recognizable treats, from blondies and brownies to bars and cookies. I've also included a couple of traditional international desserts. If you have never had Greek baklava or French madeleines, I hope you will give them a try.

Bake sales with an international theme always draw a crowd. You could offer up all of these sweets and add some of your family recipes. Or simply bake one or two and present them as fresh and exciting options. After all, it's important to occasionally land in a new place—especially when it comes to dessert!

danish "blondes"

My grandmother Hannah emigrated from Denmark and settled in Chicago. She was a wonderful baker, and her kitchen was always stocked with a glass jar of gumdrops and a big platter of warm, spicy blonde bars redolent of cloves, ginger, and cardamom. I never managed to get her exact recipe, but after years of trying, I've come up with a pretty good approximation. These humble bars are perfect for those with distinctive tastebuds. The subtle flavors entice buyers at your bake sale. The aroma from your kitchen while these are in the oven might mean making two batches—one for your family to enjoy! I usually frost this bar with Coffee-Caramel Icing (page 172).

1. Preheat the oven to 350°F. Grease a 9" x 9" baking pan with butter or cooking spray. Dust with flour and tap out the excess.

2. In a large bowl, using an electric mixer, beat the butter and sugars until light and fluffy. Beat in the eggs and the vanilla.

3. Measure the flour, baking powder, salt, cardamom, cloves, and ginger and sift directly into the butter mixture. Beat just until incorporated and no trace of the dry ingredients remains.

4. Spread the batter evenly in the prepared pan. Bake for 20 to 25 minutes, or until a toothpick inserted in the center comes out clean or with only moist crumbs, not batter, on it. The surface should be golden brown and the edges should pull away slightly from the sides of the pan. Cool in the pan on a rack for at least 1 hour. Cut into bars just before serving.

Storage: *The bars will keep longer uncut. Cover the pan with plastic wrap or foil and store at room temperature for 3 to 5 days or in the refrigerator for 6 to 8 days.*

10 tablespoons (1¼ sticks) unsalted butter, room temperature

1 cup packed light brown sugar

¼ cup granulated sugar

2 large eggs

1 teaspoon pure vanilla extract

1 cup unbleached all-purpose flour

½ teaspoon baking powder

¼ teaspoon salt

1½ teaspoons ground cardamom

½ teaspoon ground cloves

½ teaspoon ground ginger

TIP

Hand-stamped signs are easy to create! Don't worry about being perfect—imperfection is charming.

dulce de leche brownies

Dulce de leche literally means "candy of milk." Sweetened condensed milk and sugar are slowly simmered until the mixture resembles hot fudge in consistency and caramel in taste. It is extremely popular in South America, where people use it in desserts and also slather it on bread—yum! I can't imagine anything more delicious than mixing it into brownie batter. You can buy jars of dulce de leche, which is what I usually do, but I've included a recipe if you find yourself with a rainy afternoon to make the real deal (more flavorful, I confess).

DULCE DE LECHE

- 1 can (14 ounces) sweetened condensed milk
- 1 can (12 ounces) evaporated milk
- ½ teaspoon baking soda
- Big pinch of salt
- 1 tablespoon light corn syrup
- 1 teaspoon pure vanilla extract

BROWNIES

- 12 tablespoons (1½ sticks) unsalted butter
- 4 ounces bittersweet chocolate (60% or more cacao), chopped into small, even-size pieces
- 3 large eggs
- 1¼ cups granulated sugar
- 1 teaspoon pure vanilla extract
- ½ cup + 2 tablespoons unbleached all-purpose flour
- Pinch of salt

1. *To make the dulce de leche:* In a medium heavy-bottom saucepan, combine the milks. Stir in the baking soda and salt. Warm over medium-low heat, stirring constantly with a wooden spoon or a heatproof spatula, for 30 to 40 minutes, or until the mixture is deep golden brown and very thick. (If you lift the spoon and let the excess drizzle back into the pan, it should sit on the surface for at least 10 seconds before disappearing.) It's important to stir constantly. The mixture will foam at first and then thicken and bubble slowly.

2. When the dulce de leche has reached the desired consistency, remove the saucepan from the heat and let cool for 10 minutes. Stir in the corn syrup and vanilla until well combined. When the mixture has cooled completely, transfer it to a jar or bowl. You should have 1 to 1½ cups dulce de leche.

3. *To make the brownies:* Preheat the oven to 350°F. Grease a 9" x 9" baking pan with butter or cooking spray. Dust with flour and tap out the excess.

4. In a small heavy-bottom saucepan over low heat, warm the butter and chocolate, stirring frequently, until almost completely melted. Remove the saucepan from the heat and stir until smooth. Set aside and cool slightly.

5. In a large bowl, using an electric mixer, beat the eggs, sugar, and vanilla until creamy. Add the cooled chocolate mixture and mix until well combined.

6. Measure the flour and salt and sift directly into the chocolate mixture. Mix until no trace of the dry ingredients remains.

7. Spread half the brownie batter evenly into the prepared pan. Spoon ½ to ¾ cup of dulce de leche on top. (Don't worry about making it perfectly even or covering every inch!) Spread the remaining brownie batter over the dulce de leche. Using a knife or soupspoon, gently dip into the batter and pull up, making a swirled pattern over the surface.

8. Bake for 32 to 38 minutes, or until a toothpick inserted in the center comes out clean or with only crumbs, not batter, on it (a little dulce de leche is fine). Cool in the pan on a rack for at least 1 hour. Cut into bars just before serving.

Storage: *The brownies will keep longer uncut. Cover the pan with plastic wrap or foil and store in the refrigerator for 4 to 6 days.*

TIP

A tiny scoop of dulce de leche on top of a brownie is delicious.

intensely italian espresso-chocolate bars

The secret to many chocolate recipes is adding a tiny bit of coffee. Somehow it really makes the flavors pop. But I think it's a shame you can't taste it! For these brownies, I've included a whopping 3 tablespoons of espresso power. Every bite is infused with the rich, robust essence of coffee.

I love to serve these in small squares with a dollop of whipped cream on top. For your bake sale, garnish each package with store-bought chocolate-covered espresso beans. *Bella!*

---

3 tablespoons instant espresso powder

1 tablespoon very hot tap water (do not heat in the microwave oven)

4 ounces bittersweet chocolate, chopped into small, even-size pieces

10 tablespoons (1¼ sticks) unsalted butter

2 large eggs

¾ cup packed light brown sugar

¼ teaspoon pure vanilla extract

¾ cup unbleached all-purpose flour

½ teaspoon baking powder

Pinch of salt

Whipped cream (optional)

1. Preheat the oven to 350°F. Grease a 9" x 9" baking pan with butter or cooking spray. Dust with flour and tap out the excess.

2. In a small bowl, combine the espresso powder and hot water and stir until smooth. Set aside.

3. In a small heavy-bottom saucepan over low heat, warm the chocolate and butter, stirring frequently, until almost completely melted. Remove the saucepan from the heat and stir until smooth. Set aside and cool slightly.

4. In a large bowl, beat the eggs, sugar, and vanilla until creamy. Add the cooled chocolate mixture and mix until well combined. Beat in the coffee mixture.

5. Measure the flour, baking power, and salt and sift directly into the chocolate mixture. Mix until no trace of the dry ingredients remains.

6. Spread the batter into the prepared pan and bake for 30 to 33 minutes, or until a toothpick inserted in the center comes out clean or with only crumbs, not batter, on it. Cool in the pan on a rack for at least 1 hour. Cut into bars and top with whipped cream just before serving.

Storage: *The bars will keep longer uncut. Cover the pan with plastic wrap or foil and store at room temperature for 3 to 6 days or in the refrigerator for 6 to 8 days.*

swiss milk chocolate brownies

Almost every traditional brownie recipe begins with unsweetened or bittersweet chocolate. To change things up a bit, I developed this recipe using creamy, velvety Swiss milk chocolate, which is the best of its kind. No wonder Switzerland has the highest rate of chocolate consumption per capita in the world! These brownies are loaded with mountains of milk chocolate. A bit lighter and sweeter in flavor, they are an especially big hit with kids. These are divine with a slick of White Chocolate Frosting (page 173) on top.

1. Preheat the oven to 350°F. Grease a 9" x 9" baking pan with butter or cooking spray. Dust with flour and tap out the excess.

2. In a small heavy-bottom saucepan over low heat, melt the butter, unsweetened chocolate, and chopped milk chocolate, stirring frequently, until almost completely melted. Remove the saucepan from the heat and stir until smooth. Set aside and cool slightly.

3. In a large bowl, using an electric mixer, beat the eggs, sugar, and vanilla until creamy. Add the cooled chocolate mixture and mix until well combined.

4. Measure the flour and salt and sift directly into the chocolate mixture. Mix until no trace of the dry ingredients remains. Stir in the chocolate chips.

5. Using a rubber spatula, spread the batter evenly in the prepared baking pan. Bake for 25 minutes, or until a toothpick inserted in the center comes out clean or with only crumbs, not batter, on it. Cool in the pan on a rack for at least 1 hour. Cut into squares just before serving.

Storage: *The brownies will keep longer uncut. Cover the pan with plastic wrap or foil and store at room temperature for 2 to 4 days or in the refrigerator for 5 to 7 days.*

- 8 tablespoons (1 stick) unsalted butter
- 1 ounce unsweetened chocolate, chopped into small, even-size pieces
- 4 ounces milk chocolate, chopped into small, even-size pieces
- 2 large eggs
- ¾ cup granulated sugar
- 1 teaspoon pure vanilla extract
- 1 cup unbleached all-purpose flour
- ¼ teaspoon salt
- ¾ cup milk chocolate chips

chinese lucky almond cookies

It doesn't matter if it's the year of the dragon, the horse, or the monkey, offering these cookies at your bake sale is sure to bring you good fortune. The sliced almonds represent coins, so sprinkle a lot on top. If you are an almond lover like I am, these cookies are for you. The subtle flavor will bring you big winnings in taste.

8 tablespoons (1 stick) unsalted butter, room temperature

½ cup granulated sugar

1 large egg

½ teaspoon almond extract

¾ cup almond flour

¾ cup unbleached all-purpose flour

¼ teaspoon baking soda

Pinch of salt

½ cup sliced toasted almonds

TIP

If you can offer someone the chance to win a lucky gift basket of goodies (check your state's raffle regulations), it will bring excitement to the event.

1. In a large bowl, using an electric mixer, cream the butter and sugar until light and fluffy. Beat in the egg and almond extract. Add the almond flour. The dough will be crumbly.

2. Measure the all-purpose flour, baking soda, and salt and sift directly into the butter mixture. Beat until just combined. Shape the dough into a ball. Wrap in plastic wrap and transfer to the refrigerator to chill for 2 hours.

3. Preheat the oven to 350°F. Grease a large baking sheet with butter or cooking spray or line it with parchment paper.

4. Remove the dough from the refrigerator and unwrap it. Take pieces of the dough and roll them into 1" balls. Place them on the baking sheet, making sure to space them at least 1" apart. Press each ball gently with a wet thumb to flatten it slightly. Top each with some sliced almonds.

5. Bake for 10 to 14 minutes, or until the edges are slightly golden and the centers are still a bit soft. Cool on the baking sheet on a rack for 15 minutes. Remove the cookies to the rack and cool completely. Repeat with the remaining dough, if necessary.

Storage: *The cookies will keep for 5 to 7 days stored in an airtight container at room temperature.*

greek treats

Traditional Greek pastries usually involve layer upon layer of delicate phyllo dough, which is hard to make and even harder to work with. Who has the time or the patience? This baklava recipe uses pre-made and prebaked phyllo pastry shells, which can be found in the freezer section of most supermarkets. I promise, no one at your bake sale will be able to tell the difference. Just think: Instead of slaving in the kitchen, you could be relaxing on a cruise ship lounge chair watching the Mediterranean Sea float by . . . or at least putting your feet up in your own living room! If you don't care for walnuts, pistachios are a lovely alternative.

1. Preheat the oven to 350°F.

2. In a medium heavy-bottom saucepan over medium-low heat, combine the sugar and butter and stir until melted. Remove the saucepan from the heat and stir in the honey. Stir in the orange juice, orange peel, and cinnamon. Stir in the walnuts.

3. Remove the phyllo shells from the freezer and arrange them on a baking sheet lined with parchment paper. Fill each shell with the walnut mixture, overloading them just a bit.

4. Bake for 3 to 5 minutes, or until the shells are golden brown and the filling is hot. Cool on the baking sheet on a rack for 1 hour.

Storage: Cover the treats with plastic wrap or foil and store in the refrigerator for 3 to 5 days.

½ cup granulated sugar

4 tablespoons (½ stick) unsalted butter

2 tablespoons honey

3 tablespoons freshly squeezed orange juice (from 1 small orange)

1 tablespoon freshly grated orange peel

½ teaspoon ground cinnamon

1½ cups finely chopped walnuts

1 package frozen mini–phyllo shells (15–18 shells)

chocolate french madeleines

The legendary French author Marcel Proust wrote passionately about his beloved madeleines. I'm not certain how he would feel about the fact that I've added loads of chocolate to the traditional recipe, but I'm confident everyone at your bake sale will love them! Madeleines are dainty little butter cakes baked in a special pan with scallop-shaped inserts. *Très chic!* Monsieur Proust, *merci beaucoup* for writing about your childhood memories, which have claimed a place in every reader's heart.

To bake madeleines, you must have a special madeleine pan. They are inexpensive and can be found in most cooking supply stores. I promise you, the purchase is worth it. Most pans yield 12 madeleines, but there are mini-madeleine pans that yield 20. Use whichever you prefer.

8 tablespoons (1 stick) unsalted butter

3 large eggs

¾ cup granulated sugar

¾ cup all-purpose flour

¼ cup unsweetened cocoa powder

½ teaspoon baking powder

Pinch of salt

½ teaspoon pure vanilla extract

2 tablespoons confectioners' sugar (optional)

Tip Put your high school French to use and include some classic phrases—*merci beaucoup, fantastique, c'est si bon*—on your bake sale signs.

1. Preheat the oven to 375°F. Grease a madeleine pan with butter or cooking spray. Dust with flour and tap out the excess.

2. Melt the butter in a small heavy-bottom saucepan over low heat. Set aside.

3. In a large bowl, using an electric mixer, beat the eggs and granulated sugar until frothy and well blended.

4. Measure the flour, cocoa, baking powder, and salt and sift directly into the egg mixture. Beat just until combined. Beat in the melted butter and vanilla.

5. Using a soupspoon, drop mounds of batter into the madeleine pan, filling each indentation about two-thirds full. Bake for 10 to 12 minutes, or until the centers are puffed and a toothpick inserted in the center comes out clean or with only crumbs, not batter, on it. Cool in the pan on a rack for 5 to 10 minutes, or until just cool enough to handle. Remove the madeleines to the rack and cool completely. Dust with confectioners' sugar before serving, if desired.

Storage: *As soon as the madeleines have cooled (within 2 hours of baking them), transfer them to an airtight container to preserve their freshness and store at room temperature for up to 2 days.*

Tipsy Treats

Bake sales are usually thought of as kids-only affairs, but let's be honest: Does anyone ever really outgrow the need for an "after-school" snack? At Fat Witch Bakery, there is a rush every day at 4:00 p.m. A little something sweet is often just what you need to get through the end of the day. And if a fudgy brownie doesn't do the trick, a stiff drink surely will!

Why not combine the two in one? This chapter is dedicated to adults-only indulgences. It's true that bake sales often take place in the schoolyard, but they are also a great way for grown-ups to raise money—whether you are making a donation to a local charity or saving up to throw an end-of-the-season bash for your softball team. Consider organizing a bake sale at your office, your church, or your local library. Then set up a special table filled with these booze-infused treats. I promise they will sell out long before last call.

I confess that when it comes to drinking, I pretty much stick to a big glass (or two!) of red wine and skip the hard stuff. But baking is a whole other story. Liquors like rum and bourbon add depth and smoky sweetness to desserts, especially those with chocolate. Flavored liqueurs, like coconut rum, hazelnut-flavored Frangelico, and coffee-flavored Kahlúa, are a great way to enhance the flavors of sweet treats and add a little something extra that makes them even more decadent. As a bonus, a splash of booze actually improves the flavor of your dessert over time. Most of these brownies, cakes, and bars are better the next day, making them perfect bake sale fare.

Don't worry if your home bar isn't well stocked or if the bottles have been gathering dust for years. There's no need to purchase expensive tipples to make these treats—bottom-shelf brands and nip- or airplane-size bottles will do just fine. You should also feel free to experiment and make substitutions. Don't have Kahlúa? Use Baileys Irish Cream instead! Out of whiskey? Bourbon, rye, or rum will still be delicious.

rum splash banana bread

makes 10 to 12 slices

I'm about to make you very jealous. Ready? Here goes: I have cousins who live on St. Thomas in the US Virgin Islands. Family get-togethers for me are less about overstuffed turkey dinners and awkward conversations than they are about lounging on the beach with a piña colada. And instead of traditional holiday desserts, we often enjoy thick slices of this rum-spiked banana bread. It's important to use very ripe bananas (ones that are soft and covered in brown spots) because they have the most flavor. This bread can also be baked in three mini-loaf pans. Or prepare it in a 9" x 9" pan and cut into 12 to 16 squares.

1. Preheat the oven to 350°F. Grease a 9" x 5" loaf pan with butter or cooking spray. Dust with flour and tap out the excess.

2. In a large bowl, using an electric mixer, cream the butter and sugar until light and fluffy. Beat in the eggs one at a time. Beat in the rum and vanilla.

3. Measure the flour, baking soda, baking powder, salt, and cinnamon and sift directly into the butter mixture. Beat to combine. Beat in the bananas and sour cream or yogurt.

4. Spread the batter in the prepared pan and bake for 60 to 70 minutes, or until a toothpick inserted in the center comes out clean or with only moist crumbs, not batter, on it. Cool in the pan on a rack for 30 minutes. Remove to the rack and cool completely.

Storage: The banana bread will keep for 3 to 5 days covered in plastic wrap or foil and stored at room temperature.

- 8 tablespoons (1 stick) unsalted butter, room temperature
- 1 cup granulated sugar
- 2 large eggs
- ¼ cup dark rum
- 1 teaspoon pure vanilla extract
- 1½ cups unbleached all-purpose flour
- 1 teaspoon baking soda
- ½ teaspoon baking powder
- ½ teaspoon salt
- ½ teaspoon ground cinnamon
- 1 cup mashed very ripe bananas (about 2 bananas)
- ¼ cup sour cream or full-fat plain yogurt

stout gingerbread

Gingerbread can run the gamut from light, fluffy, and sweet to dark, spicy, and bitter. This version leans toward the former. Don't save this recipe for the holidays! In the summer months, I like to stir a cup of blueberries or chopped plums into the batter. This is a terrific snacking cake as is, but you can also dress it up with any of the frostings in Chapter 10. Sell it whole or cut it into squares for your bake sale. Feel free to substitute any full-bodied, flavorful beer for the stout.

2 cups unbleached all-purpose flour

1 teaspoon baking soda

1½ teaspoons ground ginger

1 teaspoon ground cinnamon

½ teaspoon ground nutmeg

¼ teaspoon salt

8 tablespoons (1 stick) unsalted butter, room temperature

¾ cup packed light brown sugar

1 large egg

¼ cup molasses

1 cup stout beer

1. Preheat the oven to 350°F. Grease a 9" x 9" baking pan with butter or cooking spray. Dust with flour and tap out the excess.

2. In a medium bowl, sift together the flour, baking soda, ginger, cinnamon, nutmeg, and salt.

3. In a large bowl, using an electric mixer, cream the butter and sugar until light and fluffy. Beat in the egg and molasses. Beat in the flour mixture alternately with the beer until just combined.

4. Spread the batter evenly into the prepared pan and bake for 35 to 40 minutes, or until a toothpick inserted in the center comes out clean or with only moist crumbs, not batter, on it. Cool in the pan on a rack. Cut into squares just before serving.

Storage: *The gingerbread will keep for 4 to 5 days covered in plastic wrap or foil and stored at room temperature.*

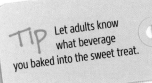

Tip Let adults know what beverage you baked into the sweet treat.

oatmeal-cider sandwich cookies

Remember oatmeal cream pies? Those snack cakes made with two incredibly soft oatmeal cookies and a slick of marshmallow cream? These are a much more delicious, much more grown-up version. A hard cider–infused buttercream frosting is sandwiched between cinnamon-scented oatmeal cookies. It's a bit like apple crisp, but you can eat it with your fingers. I love the clean, tart flavor of hard cider, but you can use regular apple cider for a nonalcoholic version.

COOKIES

- 16 tablespoons (2 sticks) unsalted butter, room temperature
- ¾ cup packed light brown sugar
- ¾ cup granulated sugar
- 2 large eggs
- 1 teaspoon pure vanilla extract
- 1½ cups unbleached all-purpose flour
- 1 teaspoon baking soda
- ½ teaspoon salt
- ½ teaspoon ground cinnamon
- 3 cups old-fashioned rolled oats

FILLING

- ½ cup hard cider
- 8 tablespoons (1 stick) unsalted butter, room temperature
- 2–3 cups confectioners' sugar

1. Preheat the oven to 350°F. Line 2 baking sheets with parchment paper.

2. *To make the cookies:* In a large bowl, using an electric mixer, beat the butter and sugars until light and fluffy. Beat in the eggs one at a time. Beat in the vanilla.

3. Measure the flour, baking soda, salt, and cinnamon and sift directly into the butter mixture. Beat to combine. Stir in the oats with a wooden spoon.

4. Using 2 soupspoons, drop balls of dough onto the prepared baking sheets, making sure to space them at least 2" apart. (You may need to work in batches.) Aim for an even number of cookies.

5. Bake for 12 to 14 minutes, or until the cookies are light golden brown and the edges are set. Cool on the baking sheets on a rack.

6. *To make the filling:* Pour the cider into a small heavy-bottom saucepan and bring to a boil over medium heat. Reduce the heat and simmer until it has reduced by half (to ¼ cup). Let the cider cool completely.

7. In a large bowl, using an electric mixer, beat the butter and 2 cups of the confectioners' sugar until smooth and creamy. Beat in the cooled cider. Gradually beat in the remaining confectioners' sugar, ½ cup at a time, until the mixture is thick and creamy.

Tip

Make half these cookies with hard cider and half with regular cider for a kid-friendly version. Make sure to label the boozy ones "Adults Only"!

8. To assemble the sandwich cookies, spread the bottom of 1 cookie with a spoonful of the filling. Top with another cookie, right side up. Repeat with the remaining cookies and filling.

Storage: *The sandwich cookies will keep 7 days stored in an airtight container at room temperature.*

milk chocolate chip biscotti with hazelnut liqueur

For some reason, I think of peanuts, walnuts, and almonds as everyday nuts and hazelnuts as fancy nuts. Perhaps that's because I associate them with the elegant Italian truffles called Baci and with Nutella, everyone's favorite gussied-up sandwich spread. These biscotti are what I bake when I'm craving something a little bit special for an after-dinner treat. Hazelnut liqueur and finely chopped hazelnuts (I pulse mine in the food processor) ensure every bite is filled with rich nutty flavor and a bit of crunch. It's a good idea to toast hazelnuts because it makes removing the skins so much easier and the end result so much tastier (see page 78). If you've never baked biscotti before, don't be shy! I promise it's no more difficult than your favorite cookie recipe. It takes just a little longer because the bars go into the oven a second time.

8 tablespoons (1 stick) unsalted butter, room temperature

¾ cup granulated sugar

2 large eggs

3 tablespoons hazelnut liqueur, such as Frangelico

2¼ cups unbleached all-purpose flour

1¼ teaspoons baking powder

¼ teaspoon salt

¾ cup finely chopped hazelnuts

¾ cup milk chocolate chips or chunks

1. In a large bowl, using an electric mixer, cream the butter and sugar until light and fluffy. Add the eggs one at a time and beat to combine. Beat in the hazelnut liqueur.

2. Measure the flour, baking powder, and salt and sift directly into the butter mixture. Beat just until combined. Stir in the hazelnuts and chocolate chips or chunks.

3. Divide the dough into 2 equal portions and wrap each half in plastic wrap. Chill in the refrigerator for at least 1 hour and up to overnight.

4. Preheat the oven to 350°F. Line a baking sheet with parchment paper.

5. Unwrap each dough half and, using floured hands, form each into a log about 12" long and 2½" wide. Place the logs on the baking sheet and bake for 30 to 35 minutes, or until light golden brown. Cool on the baking sheet on a rack for 30 minutes to 1 hour, until slightly warm.

6. Reduce the oven temperature to 300°F. With a serrated knife, cut each log diagonally into slices ½" to ¾" thick. Lay the slices flat on the baking sheet. Bake for 10 minutes, or until dry to the touch and light golden brown. Flip them over and bake for 10 minutes more. Remove the biscotti to the rack and cool completely.

Storage: *The biscotti will keep for 14 days stored in an airtight container at room temperature.*

TIp Biscotti can be baked up to a week ahead of time, then stored in an airtight container, and still be perfect for your event.

Coconut Rum
Shortbread

coconut-Rum Shortbread

A crisp, buttery, slightly salty shortbread pairs well with everything from a late-morning mug of tea to a late-night bowl of ice cream. Best of all, it couldn't be easier to bake, and most of us already have the ingredients for classic shortbread (butter, sugar, flour, salt) on hand. For this version, I add a big splash of coconut rum and a shower of shredded coconut.

1. Preheat the oven to 325°F. Line a 9" x 9" baking pan tightly with foil, extending it up the sides, and coat it with cooking spray.

2. In a large bowl, using an electric mixer, beat the butter and sugar until light and fluffy. Beat in the coconut rum.

3. Measure the flour and salt and sift directly into the butter mixture. Beat to combine. Beat in the coconut. Continue to beat until the mixture comes together as a dough.

4. With your fingers, gently pat the dough evenly into the prepared pan. Prick the dough all over with a fork. Bake for 35 to 40 minutes, or until light golden brown in the center and browned around the edges. Cool in the pan on a rack for 30 minutes, or until warm but not hot. Using the foil as handles, lift the shortbread out of the pan. Cut into squares.

Storage: *The shortbread will keep for 7 days stored in an airtight container at room temperature.*

12 tablespoons (1½ sticks) unsalted butter, room temperature

¾ cup confectioners' sugar

2 tablespoons coconut rum

1½ cups unbleached all-purpose flour

¾ teaspoon salt

½ cup shredded sweetened coconut

whiskey-walnut brownies

Plain walnut brownies are a run-of-the-mill bake sale staple. And sure, they are delicious. Crunchy walnuts, gooey chocolate—what's not to love? But I wanted to take this classic combination over the top. In this recipe, I soak the walnuts in liquor before adding them to the brownie batter. The nuts absorb all the wonderful, smoky whiskey flavors.

1 cup coarsely chopped walnuts

¼ cup whiskey

12 tablespoons (1½ sticks) unsalted butter

4 ounces bittersweet chocolate (60% cacao and up), chopped into small, even-size pieces

1¼ cups granulated sugar

3 large eggs

1 teaspoon pure vanilla extract

½ cup + 2 tablespoons unbleached all-purpose flour

Pinch of salt

1. Preheat the oven to 350°F. Grease a 9" x 9" baking pan with butter or cooking spray. Dust with flour and tap out the excess.

2. In a small mixing bowl, toss the walnuts and whiskey to combine. Set aside.

3. In a small heavy-bottom saucepan over low heat, warm the butter and chocolate, stirring frequently, until almost completely melted. Remove the saucepan from the heat and stir until smooth. Set aside and cool slightly.

4. Meanwhile, in a large bowl, beat the sugar, eggs, and vanilla until creamy. Add the cooled chocolate mixture and mix until well combined.

5. Measure the flour and salt and sift directly into the chocolate mixture. Mix gently until well combined and no trace of the dry ingredients remains. Drain the walnuts and reserve the soaking whiskey. Stir the walnuts into the batter and add 2 tablespoons of the soaking whiskey.

6. Spread the batter evenly in the prepared pan and bake for 30 to 35 minutes, or until a toothpick inserted in the center comes out clean or with only moist crumbs, not batter, on it. Cool in the pan on a rack for 1 hour. Cut into squares just before serving.

Storage: *The brownies will keep longer uncut. Cover the pan with plastic wrap or foil and store at room temperature for 4 to 5 days or in the refrigerator for 6 to 8 days.*

citrus squares with orange liqueur

makes 12 to 16 bars

There is an adage that suggests you are either a chocolate person or a lemon person. Clearly, chocolate comes first in my heart! But I have a soft spot for lemon squares, too. This recipe is a riff on the classic version. I've kept the crumbly, buttery shortbread crust, but I amped up the flavor of the filling with lime juice and orange liqueur, which provide slightly warm, boozy undertones. These look extra pretty sprinkled with a bit of confectioners' sugar before serving.

CRUST

- 1 cup unbleached all-purpose flour
- ½ cup confectioners' sugar
- ¼ teaspoon salt
- 8 tablespoons (1 stick) unsalted butter, finely chopped

FILLING

- 1½ cups granulated sugar
- ¼ cup unbleached all-purpose flour
- ¼ teaspoon salt
- 3 large eggs
- 3 tablespoons freshly squeezed lemon juice (1 lemon)
- 2 teaspoons lemon peel (finely grated lemon)
- 3 tablespoons freshly squeezed lime juice + 1 teaspoon lime peel (from 1–2 limes)
- 2 tablespoons orange liqueur, such as Grand Marnier
- Confectioners' sugar

1. Line a 9" x 9" baking pan with parchment paper, making sure that it extends up all the sides.

2. *To make the crust:* In a large bowl, combine the flour, sugar, and salt. Using an electric mixer, beat in the butter a few pieces at a time until well incorporated. The mixture should look like coarse crumbs. Press the mixture evenly into the bottom of the prepared pan. Put the pan in the freezer for 15 minutes.

3. Preheat the oven to 350°F.

4. When the crust is well chilled, bake for 20 minutes, or until light golden brown. Cool the pan completely on a rack. Leave the oven on.

5. *To make the filling:* In a large bowl, combine the sugar, flour, salt, eggs, lemon juice and peel, lime juice and peel, and orange liqueur. Beat with an electric mixer until smooth.

6. Pour the filling over the crust and bake for 30 to 35 minutes,

or until the filling is set in the center. Cool completely in the pan on a rack, then transfer to the refrigerator to chill. Using the parchment paper as handles, lift the entire square out of the pan and cut into bars. Dust with confectioners' sugar just before serving.

Storage: *The squares will keep longer uncut. Cover the pan with plastic wrap or foil and store in the refrigerator for 3 to 5 days.*

TIP

Since confectioners' sugar can "melt" off baked goods, have a fine-mesh sieve on hand at your bake sale. That way you can dust your treats at the last minute, ensuring a perfect presentation and exciting performance. Don't stack these goodies.

Kahlúa-chocolate chip cookies

Everyone has his or her own version of the perfect chocolate chip cookie. This one is mine: thin and crispy around the edges with a thick, soft middle, a hint of brown sugar, and loads of semisweet chocolate chips. Oh, and did I forget to mention a shot of Kahlúa? The coffee liqueur enhances the chocolate and gives these cookies incredible flavor.

- 16 tablespoons (2 sticks) unsalted butter, room temperature
- ¾ cup packed light brown sugar
- ¾ cup granulated sugar
- 2 large eggs
- 2 tablespoons Kahlúa or other coffee-flavored liqueur
- ½ teaspoon pure vanilla extract
- 2 tablespoons instant coffee granules
- 2½ cups all-purpose flour
- 1 teaspoon baking soda
- ¾ teaspoon salt
- 1½ cups semisweet chocolate chips

1. In a large bowl, using an electric mixer, cream the butter and sugars until light and fluffy. Add the eggs one at a time and beat to combine. Add the Kahlúa, vanilla, and coffee granules (if using) and continue to beat until smooth and well combined.

2. Measure the flour, baking soda, and salt and sift directly into the batter. Mix well until no trace of the dry ingredients remains. Stir in the chocolate chips. Chill the dough in the refrigerator for 20 minutes.

3. Preheat the oven to 350°F. Grease 2 large baking sheets with butter or cooking spray or line them with parchment paper.

4. Using 2 soupspoons, drop balls of dough onto the prepared baking sheets, making sure to space them at least 2" apart. Bake for 10 to 12 minutes, or until the edges are crisp and the centers are no longer shiny. Cool on the baking sheets on a rack for at least 20 minutes. Remove the cookies to a serving platter and cool completely. Repeat with the remaining cookie dough.

Storage: *The cookies will keep for up to 7 days stored in an airtight container at room temperature.*

over-the-top icings

Even though I live in New York City, the fashion capital of the USA, I don't like to dress up. Sure, I love strolling down Madison Avenue and admiring the designer dresses, shoes, and handbags in the store windows, but when it comes to my own clothes, give me jeans and a cozy sweater any day. On the rare occasion that I have a formal event, I always fall back on the same outfit: a black silk pantsuit topped off with my pearl and jade necklace. It's classic and timeless.

Like my taste in clothes, my taste in desserts is similarly understated. I gravitate toward comforting, homey treats that need little or no adornment—like brownies. They are simply perfect straight out of the pan and best eaten with your fingers. But there are times when a little extra glitz and glamour (or butter and sugar!) are needed. A bake sale is a perfect example. Brownies and blondies are enticing on their own, but they will really fly

165

off the sale table when topped with an icing like coffee caramel, peanut butter, or Baileys chocolate.

The recipes in this chapter are a snap to prepare—no double boilers or candy thermometers required. I've made pairing suggestions (the Maple Icing on the Bacon Brownies is a must!), but you should, of course, feel free to use your imagination. What's the difference between frosting and icing? This is one of life's great questions. I've never known the answer, so I use the terms interchangeably.

basic chocolate frosting

Like diamond studs or a gold watch, this simple chocolate frosting is a classic. It's a great way to "accessorize" any dessert. I often use it to top off Peanut Butter Brownies (page 42) and Whiskey-Walnut Brownies (page 158). A little dab on Chinese Lucky Almond Cookies (page 138) is complex and delicious, too.

After you spread the frosting on your dessert, put the pan in the refrigerator for about an hour to allow it to set.

---

4 tablespoons (½ stick) unsalted butter, chopped

4 ounces bittersweet chocolate, chopped into small, even-size pieces

3 tablespoons half-and-half

1 teaspoon pure vanilla extract

1 cup confectioners' sugar

1. In a small heavy-bottom saucepan over low heat, warm the butter and chocolate, stirring frequently, until almost completely melted. Remove the saucepan from the heat and stir until smooth. Whisk in the half-and-half and vanilla. Measure the sugar and sift directly into the pan. Whisk until well combined and smooth, about 2 minutes.

2. Spread the frosting on cooled brownies, bars, or cookies. Transfer to the refrigerator to set the frosting. Cut brownies or bars into squares just before serving.

buttercream perfection

Fluffy, sweet buttercream is a must for topping layer cakes and cupcakes—and the more the better! I like to mound on big, billowy clouds. This is my go-to vanilla frosting recipe. Experiment by adding drops of different extracts, liqueurs, bits of chocolate, or nuts, or toss on sprinkles and candy after the icing is on the pastry.

This is perfect on Chocolate Layer Cake (page 25) and Birthday Cake (page 50). Slather some on Baby Brownie Cupcakes (page 32) and, with a fork, drizzle it on Intensely Italian Espresso-Chocolate Bars (page 136).

1. In a medium bowl, using an electric mixer on medium speed, cream the butter and vanilla until smooth. Measure ¾ cup of the sugar and sift directly into the butter mixture. Beat until smooth. Sift in the remaining ¼ cup sugar alternately with the half-and-half and beat until light and fluffy.

2. Spread the frosting on cooled brownies, bars, cakes, or cookies. Transfer to the refrigerator to set the frosting. Cut brownies or bars into squares just before serving.

4 tablespoons (½ stick) unsalted butter, room temperature

1 teaspoon pure vanilla extract

1 cup confectioners' sugar, divided

2 tablespoons half-and-half

cream cheese schmear

The famous package might say Philadelphia, but cream cheese was actually invented in New York. Its silky texture and subtle tang make it a perfect topping for bagels, of course, and also a great base for dessert icings. I love to "schmear" it on Red Velvet–Milk Chocolate Brownies (page 31), Danish "Blondes" (page 133), and any breakfast-inspired treat, like Snooze Bars (page 72).

4 ounces cream cheese, room temperature

3 tablespoons unsalted butter, room temperature

1 teaspoon pure vanilla extract

1¼ cups confectioners' sugar

1. In a medium bowl, using an electric mixer, beat the cream cheese and butter until smooth. Beat in the vanilla. Measure the sugar and sift directly into the butter mixture. Beat until thick and creamy.

2. Spread the frosting on cooled brownies, bars, or cookies. Transfer to the refrigerator to set the frosting. Cut brownies or bars into squares just before serving.

maple icing

Here's an icing that would make Paul Bunyan smile. While adding frosting to a stack of flapjacks first thing in the morning would be a little much even for me, this icing is absolutely delicious on breakfast-y desserts like Pancake Cookies (page 83) and Bacon Brownies (page 119). It's also delicious spread across Swiss Milk Chocolate Brownies (page 137). You must use real maple syrup here, not the imitation flavoring.

1. In a medium bowl, using an electric mixer on medium speed or a big wooden spoon, beat the butter until smooth. Measure ¾ cup of the sugar and sift directly into the butter mixture. Beat until smooth. Sift in the remaining ¼ cup sugar alternately with the maple syrup and beat until the icing is light and fluffy.

2. Spread the frosting on cooled brownies, bars, or cookies. Transfer to the refrigerator to set the frosting. Cut brownies or bars into squares just before serving.

4 tablespoons (½ stick) unsalted butter, room temperature

1 cup confectioners' sugar

3 tablespoons pure maple syrup

coffee-caramel icing

Coffee and caramel might seem like an unlikely combination, but trust me: This icing is absolutely incredible. Rich roasted coffee and smooth caramel pair wonderfully with chocolate, so this is a natural choice for Chocolate French Madeleines (page 142). I particularly like it on top of Cayenne-Coffee Brownies (page 126), and I almost always use it to ice Danish "Blondes" (page 133). It's definitely worth adding a dollop between 2 Kahlúa–Chocolate Chip Cookies (page 162).

4 tablespoons (½ stick) unsalted butter

½ cup packed light brown sugar

1 teaspoon instant coffee crystals

2 tablespoons half-and-half

½ teaspoon pure vanilla extract

1 cup confectioners' sugar

1. Warm the butter in a small heavy-bottom saucepan over low heat until almost completely melted. Using a heatproof spatula, stir in the brown sugar and coffee crystals until well combined. Remove the saucepan from the heat and stir in the half-and-half and vanilla. Measure the confectioners' sugar and sift directly into the saucepan. Stir until smooth and creamy. Allow the frosting to cool for 10 minutes.

2. Spread the frosting on cooled brownies, bars, or cookies. Transfer to the refrigerator to set the frosting. Cut brownies or bars into squares just before serving.

white chocolate frosting

If you are one of those people who turn up their noses at white chocolate, then you have probably never tasted the good stuff. High-quality white chocolate has a rich, milky taste and silky texture that is perfect for frosting. This is especially dramatic paired with dark chocolate treats, like Turbo-Chocolate Cookies (page 27). It is also delicious spread over Coconut–Macadamia Nut Cookies (page 67), and I sometimes coat Chocolate French Madeleines (page 142) with it.

1. In a small heavy-bottom saucepan over low heat, melt the white chocolate chips and butter, stirring frequently. (Be very careful, as white chocolate burns easily.) When almost completely melted, remove the saucepan from the heat and stir until smooth. Whisk in the half-and-half and vanilla. Measure the sugar and sift directly into the saucepan. Whisk until smooth.

2. Spread the frosting on cooled brownies, bars, or cookies. Transfer to the refrigerator to set the frosting. Cut brownies or bars into squares just before serving.

½ cup best-quality white chocolate chips

3 tablespoons unsalted butter, chopped

2 tablespoons half-and-half

1 teaspoon pure vanilla extract

1 cup confectioners' sugar

pb frosting

What's that you say? You've never snuck a spoon into a jar of peanut butter and then licked it clean? I don't believe you. A giant spoonful of peanut butter, preferably eaten while standing alone in the kitchen in the middle of the night, is one of life's great pleasures. It was also the inspiration for this frosting. I like to dab some over Thumbprint Blondies with Jam (page 41), use it to top off Baby Brownie Cupcakes (page 32), and spread it over Yogurt Brownies (page 59). Use peanut butter without added salt or sugar, if possible.

¾ cup peanut butter

2 tablespoons unsalted butter, room temperature

½ teaspoon pure vanilla extract

1½ cups confectioners' sugar

1. In a medium bowl, using an electric mixer, cream the peanut butter and butter until smooth. Beat in the vanilla. Measure the sugar and sift directly into the butter mixture. Beat until smooth and creamy.

2. Using a tablespoon or spatula, spread the icing over cooled brownies, bars, or cookies. If desired, use a fork to make a cross-hatch pattern over the top. Transfer to the refrigerator to set the frosting. Cut brownies or bars into squares just before serving.

cinnamon icing

A crown of cinnamon icing adds spicy, fiery flavor to desserts. Of course, it's a natural pairing with gingery treats, but don't be afraid to think outside the spice jar. I love it on top of Sweet Potato Brownies (page 68) or dabbed on Pancake Cookies (page 83).

1. In a medium bowl, using an electric mixer, cream the butter and granulated sugar until light and fluffy. Measure the confectioners' sugar and cinnamon and sift directly into the butter mixture. Beat until smooth and creamy.

2. Spread the frosting on cooled brownies, bars, or cookies. Transfer to the refrigerator to set the frosting. Cut brownies or bars into squares just before serving.

4 tablespoons (½ stick) unsalted butter, room temperature
¼ cup granulated sugar
⅔ cup confectioners' sugar
1 teaspoon ground cinnamon

Baileys chocolate icing

A big splash of Baileys Irish Cream liqueur over ice is almost dessert in and of itself. Note the word *almost*. Baileys is so delicious, why limit your consumption to an after-dinner drink? Trust me, it's even better when combined with chocolate and whipped into a rich, buttery icing. I love a dab of this on Turbo-Chocolate Cookies (page 27). It also makes a great dip for Chocolate French Madeleines (page 142). Throw caution (and calorie counts) to the wind and spread it over Pecan Bars (page 60). Because of the alcohol, be sure to label any treats topped with this icing as "adults only" at your bake sale.

4 tablespoons (½ stick) unsalted butter

1 ounce bittersweet chocolate, chopped into small, even-size pieces

¼ cup Baileys Irish Cream liqueur

1 cup confectioners' sugar

1. In a small heavy-bottom saucepan over low heat, warm the butter and chocolate, stirring frequently, until almost completely melted. Remove the saucepan from the heat and stir until smooth. Whisk in the Baileys. Measure the sugar and sift directly into the saucepan. Whisk to combine. The icing should be very smooth.

2. Spread the frosting on cooled brownies, bars, or cookies. Transfer to the refrigerator to set the frosting. Cut brownies or bars into squares just before serving.

acknowledgments

Nobody does anything alone. I thank all the people who helped me with this cook-book. Much appreciation goes to Dervla Kelly, a wonderful and patient editor; Sharon Bowers, my agent, who never failed to be supportive; and Lucy Baker, who always made the manuscript better. A special tip of the hat to Alexandra Grablewski, a genius photographer (who serves the best tea); Yusef McLemore for helping with the styling; and Allison Benyo, who went above and beyond testing recipes. And I would like to thank my fabulous Fat Witch staff; each and every one of them always has a smile and outstanding work ethic.

Index

Boldface page numbers indicate photographs.

C

conversion chart

VOLUME MEASUREMENTS			WEIGHT MEASUREMENTS		LENGTH MEASUREMENTS	
U.S.	IMPERIAL	METRIC	U.S.	METRIC	U.S.	METRIC
¼ tsp	–	1 ml	1 oz	30 g	¼"	0.6 cm
½ tsp	–	2 ml	2 oz	60 g	½"	1.25 cm
1 tsp	–	5 ml	4 oz (¼ lb)	115 g	1"	2.5 cm
1 Tbsp	–	15 ml	5 oz (⅓ lb)	145 g	2"	5 cm
2 Tbsp (1 oz)	1 fl oz	30 ml	6 oz	170 g	4"	11 cm
¼ cup (2 oz)	2 fl oz	60 ml	7 oz	200 g	6"	15 cm
⅓ cup (3 oz)	3 fl oz	80 ml	8 oz (½ lb)	230 g	8"	20 cm
½ cup (4 oz)	4 fl oz	120 ml	10 oz	285 g	10"	25 cm
⅔ cup (5 oz)	5 fl oz	160 ml	12 oz (¾ lb)	340 g	12" (1')	30 cm
¾ cup (6 oz)	6 fl oz	180 ml	14 oz	400 g		
1 cup (8 oz)	8 fl oz	240 ml	16 oz (1 lb)	455 g		
			2.2 lb	1 kg		

PAN SIZES		TEMPERATURES		
U.S.	METRIC	FAHRENHEIT	CENTIGRADE	GAS
8" cake pan	20 × 4 cm sandwich or cake tin	140°	60°	–
9" cake pan	23 × 3.5 cm sandwich or cake tin	160°	70°	–
		180°	80°	–
11" × 7" baking pan	28 × 18 cm baking tin	225°	105°	¼
13" × 9" baking pan	32.5 × 23 cm baking tin	250°	120°	½
15" × 10" baking pan	38 × 25.5 cm baking tin (Swiss roll tin)	275°	135°	1
		300°	150°	2
1 ½-qt baking dish	1.5-liter baking dish	325°	160°	3
2-qt baking dish	2-liter baking dish	350°	180°	4
2-qt rectangular baking dish	30 × 19 cm baking dish	375°	190°	5
		400°	200°	6
9" pie plate	22 × 4 or 23 × 4 cm pie plate	425°	220°	7
7" or 8" springform pan	18- or 20-cm springform or loose-bottom cake tin	450°	230°	8
		475°	245°	9
9" × 5" loaf pan	23 × 13 cm or 2-lb narrow loaf tin or pâté tin	500°	260°	–